AIR BATTLE CENTRAL EUROPE

OTHER BOOKS BY ALFRED PRICE

Instruments of Darkness
Aircraft Versus Submarine
Battle Over The Reich
Blitz on Britain
The Spitfire Story
Battle of Britain: The Hardest Day
Harrier at War

WITH JEFF ETHELL

Air War South Atlantic
The German Jets in Combat
Target Berlin

AIR BATTLE CENTRAL EUROPE

ALFRED PRICE

THE FREE PRESS
A Division of Macmillan, Inc.
New York

The author and publisher are grateful to the following for providing and granting permission to reproduce the photographs between pages 80 and 81:

1, RAF; 2, Col. Robson; 3, Boeing; 4 and 5, USAF; 6, RAF; 7, RNAF; 8, 9, 10 and 11, USAF; 12 and 13, RAF; 14, 15 and 16, Panavia; 17 and 18, German Air Force; 19 and 20, Panavia; 21 and 22, author; 23, Air Cdr Johns; 24, 25, 26 and 27, USAF; 28, RAF; 29, RNAF; 30, 31 and 32, Westland; 33, Lt-Col. Hyde-Smith; 34, 35, 36 and 37, USAF; 38 and 39, Panavia; 40 FKpt Liche; 41 and 42, Panavia; 43, RAF; 44, Dassault-Breguet; 45, RNAF; 46, Hunting Engineering.

The Free Press
A Division of Macmillan, Inc.
866 Third Avenue, New York, N.Y. 10022

First American Edition 1987

Printed in the United States of America

printing number

1 2 3 4 5 6 7 8 9 10

All maps and diagrams by John Ridyard

Library of Congress Cataloging-in-Publication Data

Price, Alfred.
  Air battle Central Europe.

  Includes index.
  1. Air forces—Europe. 2. North Atlantic Treaty
Organization—Armed Forces. 3. Warsaw Treaty
Organization—Armed Forces. 4. Air warfare. I. Title.
UG635.E85P75 1987   358.4'148   87-89
ISBN 0-02-925451-5

'Air Power is a thunderbolt launched from an egg-shell invisibly tethered to a base.'

– HOFFMAN NICKERSON

CONTENTS

Preface

Numerous books have been published which purport to describe 'air power', but in many cases they are straight regurgitations of material from aircraft and weapon manufacturers' brochures plus a sprinkling of jargon words and acronyms, which give little or no idea of where the various systems fit into 'the big picture'.

Air Battle Central Europe is different. In this book I have described the most concentrated air action I can imagine: that over and around a full-scale land battle on the flatlands of northern Germany, during the non-nuclear phase of a major conflict between NATO and Warsaw Pact forces taking place between 1986 and 1990. I have avoided any attempt to describe events after the nuclear threshold has been crossed, because nuclear attacks on airfields would almost certainly bring most of the tactical air battle to an immediate end.

To assemble this account I interviewed several NATO officers, asking them to explain in non-technical language how they would direct the air forces under their command in time of war. The dictates of security did not allow the officers to tell all, but I believe that what they have said is accurate and their opinions are relevant opinions. Chapters based on fifteen of these interviews form the body of this book. These personal accounts tell the story in a way that is credible and understandable, and they show clearly how widely differing elements of air power come together to form a complex whole. The accounts also convey a spine-chilling vision of the horrors that would result from even a non-nuclear air war in Central Europe.

I am extremely grateful to the very busy men who kindly gave me their time and their views to make this book possible: Air Marshal Sir Patrick Hine; Air Vice Marshal Ken Hayr; Air Commodore Dick Johns; Colonel Keith Robson; Wing Commander Grant McLeod; Lieutenant-Colonels Tom Lyon, Carl Loveland, Les Kersey, David Vesely, Peter Granger, Paul Fazackerley and Wilfred Hyde-Smith; Oberstleutnant Walter Jertz, Fregattenkapitaen Volke Liche and Major Charles Casey. The account which follows depends heavily on the views of these interviewees, but I alone am responsible for those opinions not attributed to anyone else.

I am also grateful to the members of the various services' public relations staffs and others who arranged the interviews. In particular I should like to acknowledge valuable assistance from the following: Air Commodore R. Robson, Director of Public Relations (RAF), and his deputy, Michael Pentreath, Peter Hicks at Headquarters RAF Germany, Captains Yaple and Fraize at Headquarters Third US Air Division, Captain Lamp at Upper Heyford, Jim Sherman at Headquarters US Air Forces Europe, Air Commodore C. Reineck at the British Embassy at Bonn, Oberst W. Geissinger at the German Embassy in London and Brigadier C. Jebens at Army Air Corps Headquarters at Netheravon. I am also grateful to Air Commodore Henry Probert and Marjorie Parks at the Air Historical Branch in London for their help and understanding.

Finally, I should like to thank John Ridyard for drawing the maps and diagrams, and Aerospace Publishing for permission to use their drawings of Harrier operating sites.

February 1986

ALFRED PRICE,
Uppingham,
Rutland,
England

Author's Note

In this book distances are given in nautical miles; 1 nautical mile =
1.15 statute miles = 1.85 km. Aircraft speeds are given in knots;
1 knot = 1 nautical mile per hour. The speed of sound, Mach 1, is
approximately 660 knots at sea level. Aircraft weights are quoted in
long tons (2,240 lb = 1.018 tonnes).

At air displays it is fashionable to set around a combat aircraft
every type of weapon it can possibly carry. And manufacturers'
publicity photographs often show aircraft carrying weapon loads
far greater than they could possibly carry any useful distance in
time of war. Where aircraft bomb loads are discussed or depicted in
this book, they are in each case representative war loads that would
be carried in action by the type of aircraft described.

List of Maps, Diagrams and Drawings

Prologue

Communiqué No.1
Headquarters 2nd Allied Tactical Air Force
2300 hours GMT

AIR SUPPORT LAND BATTLE IN NORTHERN GERMANY
No Use of Nuclear Weapons by Either Side

Shortly before 0400 hours GMT this morning Warsaw Pact forces crossed the inner German border in force at several points and advanced into the area defended by the Northern Army Group. The main lines of advance are to the north and south of Brunswick, and to the north of Kassel. Simultaneously waves of enemy aircraft, some with fighter escorts, fanned out over West Germany and attacked targets there and in Holland and Belgium with high-explosive and chemical weapons. Surface-to-surface missiles with chemical warheads were launched at other targets. There are no reports of nuclear weapons having been used. The attacks caused widespread damage and casualties. Several of the enemy formations were intercepted by F-4, F-15 and F-16 fighters of the US, British, German, Dutch and Belgian Air Forces, in many cases directed by Airborne Warning and Control System (AWACS) aircraft. The enemy air attacks continued throughout the period under review and there were numerous air combats.

Up to 2200 hours GMT, 2 ATAF fighters operating in the defensive role had destroyed 281 aircraft and probably destroyed 35 others, and forced many to jettison their loads clear of targets; surface-to-air missile batteries were also in action and shot down 162 enemy aircraft and probably destroyed 22 more.

Before dawn 2 ATAF fighters, F-15s of the US Air Force and F-4s of the German Air Force, provided cover for German Navy Tornadoes which attacked a concentration of enemy shipping near the island of Rügen in the Baltic. The fighters broke up attempts by enemy aircraft to interfere with the attack, and destroyed 12 and probably destroyed 5 more. The attack on the ships was successful and there were a number of hits with air-to-surface missiles; at least three ships are stopped dead in the water, others were sunk and the remainder withdrew to the east. It is believed that an attempt has been frustrated to launch an amphibious landing operation on NATO territory.

At first light the enemy launched a large-scale helicopter assault operation to seize bridges over the Weser river, south of Bremen. While F-16s of the Dutch and Belgian Air Forces held off the enemy fighter escort, German Air Force Alphajets made repeated attacks on the transport helicopters and destroyed 41 and probably destroyed 6 more. Severe casualites were caused among troops on board the helicopters. During air combats in the area 6 enemy fixed-winged aircraft were destroyed and another 2 probably destroyed. Later in the morning 2 ATAF fighters mounted a covering operation while Allied transport helicopters flew troops into positions to seal off the pocket.

Good weather over the combat area until late in the afternoon assisted 2 ATAF to mount an effective programme of attacks aimed at slowing the enemy thrusts, giving time for Allied ground forces to move into blocking positions. From first light relays of US Air Force A-10 aircraft flew attack missions against advancing enemy troops on all three lines of thrust, in some cases against armoured units whose leading elements were in contact with Allied ground forces. The A-10s destroyed 1,035 tanks and armoured vehicles, plus 4 aircraft and helicopters which they encountered during their operations. In several cases American, British and German Army anti-tank helicopter units launched attacks co-ordinated with those of the A-10s. By the late afternoon low cloud drifting in from the west, combined with the pall of smoke and dust from the many fires and explosions, forced an end to close support operations by fixed-winged aircraft against the enemy armoured thrusts. But by then strong Allied troop reinforcements were in position to block the enemy advances.

The first 2 ATAF aircraft in action over enemy territory were Harriers of the Royal Air Force, operating from dispersed sites near the battle area. They were soon joined by Mirage, NF-5 and Alphajet attack aircraft of the Belgian, Dutch and German Air Forces. Throughout the daylight hours large forces of these attack aircraft, in some cases escorted by fighters and electronic warfare support aircraft, bombed and strafed concentrations of enemy vehicles on roads leading to the battle area. More than 2,000 vehicles were destroyed during these actions; because of dense smoke rising from the many burning vehicles in the areas attacked, it is not possible to give a more exact estimate of the number destroyed. Enemy fighters attempted to interfere with these operations and several air combats developed, during which 17 enemy aircraft were destroyed and 6 probably destroyed.

During the late afternoon the spell of good weather came to an end, and low cloud and then darkness provided ideal conditions for 2 ATAF night and all-weather attack aircraft, F-111s of the US Air Force and Tornadoes of the British and German Air Forces, to carry the war deep into enemy territory. A number of attacks were mounted against road and rail communications, command and control facilities, airfields and other important targets well behind the battle area. In some cases these attacks were supported by fighters and defence suppression aircraft. During these operations 8 enemy aircraft were destroyed and 3 probably destroyed.

Throughout the period 2 ATAF tactical reconnaissance aircraft – RF-4s, F-16s, Jaguars, Mirages, Harriers and Alphajets – flew a large number of sorties to gather information on enemy troop movements and the effects of air attacks.

During the air fighting up to 2200 hours GMT, a total of 68 aircraft of 2 ATAF had failed to return from operational sorties.

A large-scale operation is in progress to reinforce 2 ATAF with units from the United Kingdom and the USA. Numerous combat aircraft have arrived and are continuing to arrive in the theatre, and some of these have already flown in action.

———————

If Warsaw Pact forces ever launched a thrust into NATO territory, that communiqué might be issued some hours later by Headquarters 2nd Allied Tactical Air Force (2 ATAF). But behind the bland official language, what might have been the reality of such an air battle? For a large-scale action of this kind it is to be expected that there would be exaggerations in the losses claimed to have been inflicted on the enemy, in some cases by factors of the order of two or three. Beyond that, what influence might air power exert on a land battle of this sort? Indeed, is it likely that such an action would ever occur? In an effort to find the answers to these questions and to discover the 'shape' such an air battle might take, this author interviewed fifteen middle-ranking and high-ranking officers who hold or have recently held posts directing air units earmarked to support NATO operations in Central Europe. Accounts based on these interviews make up the chapters which follow.

The narrative of this book is centred on the 2nd Allied Tactical Air Force, comprising Royal Air Force and US, German, Belgian and Dutch Air Force units, which would conduct the majority of air operations that would take place over and around a land battle in Northern Germany; most of those interviewed held command posts either at the headquarters or in units assigned to 2 ATAF. The US Air Force units operating EF-111 jamming escort aircraft and F-4G defence suppression aircraft are not part of 2 ATAF, but their aircraft and crews would come under its control to support specific operations in time of war. The Lynx anti-tank helicopter unit described is an integral part of a British Army armoured brigade and therefore outside 2 ATAF control, though its helicopters would operate in the 2 ATAF area; in this context the anti-tank helicopters are treated as land vehicles (given the way they would operate, that is only a few feet from reality). Finally, to broaden the picture and to show that 2 ATAF would not operate in isolation, there are descriptions of the German Navy's Marine Flieger Geschwader 1 whose Tornado aircraft would fly anti-ship missions over the Baltic, and No.11 Group of the Royal Air Force responsible for the air defence of the United Kingdom and the surrounding sea areas.

In each case the interviewees were asked how their units might go into action using the equipment currently available. The interviews took place between the autumn of 1984 and the summer of 1985. The units described were those with the most modern aircraft and weapons deployed in Europe at the time of writing. No new types of aircraft and few new types of weapon are scheduled to enter service in the units described before 1990. So unless there is a major shift in military or political policy, it is unlikely that the composition or the capability of NATO air force units in the area will alter significantly before the end of the decade.

1: View from the Top

Currently commander of NATO's 2nd Allied Tactical Air Force (2 ATAF), Air Marshal Sir Patrick 'Paddy' Hine joined the Royal Air Force in 1950. His first tour as a fighter pilot was with No. 1 Squadron flying Meteors, after which he spent three years as a flying instructor. In 1957 he joined No. 111 Squadron and flew Hunters with the famous 'Black Arrows' aerobatic team. In 1962 he took command of No. 92 Squadron, initially equipped with Hunters and later with Lightnings. Then came a spell in staff positions, followed in 1970 by the command of No. 17 Squadron flying Phantoms in the ground attack role. After promotion to Group Captain he commanded the important base at Wildenrath in Germany, which then operated three squadrons of Harriers. Following this he moved through a series of further staff posts before, in April 1983, he took up his present command which includes all Royal Air Force units in Germany.

Under normal peacetime conditions 2 ATAF operates a total of some 725 fast-jet aircraft, drawn in roughly equal proportions from the Royal Air Force and the US, Dutch, Belgian and German Air Forces. At the time of writing, the multi-national force comprises the following units:

Interceptor Fighters
  1 squadron of F-15s (USAF)
  4 squadrons of Phantoms (RAF and German AF)
  1 squadron of F-16s (Belgian AF)
Interceptor Fighter/Attack Aircraft
  6 squadrons of F-16s (Belgian and Dutch AFs)
Medium/Long-Range Attack Aircraft
  2 squadrons of F-4s (German AF)
  7 squadrons of Tornadoes (RAF and German AF)
  3 squadrons of F-111s (USAF)

Short-Range Attack Aircraft
  4 squadrons of NF-5s (Dutch AF)
  2 squadrons of Harriers (RAF; one of these also operates in
    the battlefield reconnaissance role)
  3 squadrons of A-10s (USAF)
  2 squadrons of Alphajets (German AF)
  3 squadrons of Mirage 5s (Belgian AF)
Specialized Reconnaissance Aircraft
  1 squadron of RF-4 Phantoms (USAF)
  1 squadron of F-16s (Dutch AF)
  1 squadron of Jaguars (RAF)
  1 squadron of Mirages (Belgian AF)
  1 squadron of Alphajets (Belgian AF, visual reconnaissance
    only)

Apart from the USAF F-111, A-10 and RF-4 Phantom reconnaissance units, which are normally based in England, all units
assigned to 2 ATAF are based at airfields on the continent of
Europe; and, when required, the A-10 force could move rapidly
to its assigned forward bases in Germany. In addition to his own
forces, the Commander of 2 ATAF can call on the Commander
Allied Air Forces Central Europe for the use of special-purpose
units under his control: E-3 airborne warning and control system
(AWACS) aircraft, KC-135 flight refuelling tanker aircraft,
EF-111 electronic warfare escort aircraft and F-4 'Wild Weasel'
defence suppression aircraft.

During a period of tension 2 ATAF could expect a reinforcement of between 370 and 550 combat aircraft, depending on the
demands of other theatres of operations. Most of the reinforcing
units would come from the USA, though some would be
home-based RAF units. In total this adds up to a large number
of aircraft, but is the number large enough? How does it measure
up against the threat?

'If we received all the reinforcement aircraft that are assigned
to us, they would nearly double the strength of my force. Is
that enough? Put it this way, in terms of combat aircraft we
are currently outnumbered by about 2.3 to 1 by the Warsaw
Pact air force units in place in the central region of Europe. In

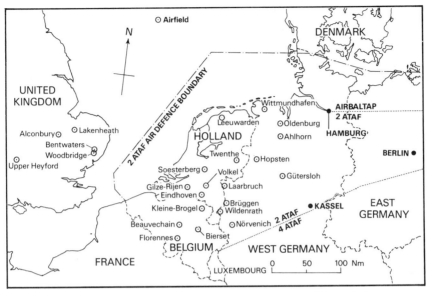

2 ATAF area of operations and main airfields. South of Kassel air operations are controlled by 4 ATAF; to the north west, air defence is the responsibility of No. 11 Group of the RAF; north of Hamburg air attack operations are controlled by AIRBALTAP (Air Forces Baltic Approaches) but 2 ATAF is responsible for air defence up to the Danish border

a time of increased tension or conflict we would receive reinforcements. But reinforcement works both ways, and I would expect the Warsaw Pact forces to receive reinforcements too and they can reinforce their front line units quicker than we can. That concerns me, because in any conflict it would give the enemy air commander a head start. Therefore we have to make up for the difference in quantity with quality. I believe that the quality of our equipment is in many respects better than that made in the Soviet Union, particularly our aero-engines and electronics; and I also believe that the quality of our crews and our tactics and operating procedures are better.'

The Commander then went on to outline the ways in which 2 ATAF might be used in time of war:

'The main tasks of my force in any major war in the Central Region would be twofold: first counter-air operations, to do our best to prevent the enemy air force attacking our ground troops and our airfields; and secondly offensive air support operations, to provide tactical reconnaissance, close support for the land battle and missions to interdict – to cut off – the battle area from enemy reinforcing units which would otherwise go into action during the next twenty-four or thirty-six hours.

Now, to do those things effectively, we have to keep our own air bases open. Since NATO is a defensive alliance it is inconceivable that we would be allowed to attack the Warsaw Pact airfields before their forces attacked us. So I work on the basis that I would have to absorb the first intensive air attacks by the enemy against us. If I were the Warsaw Pact air commander and had been given political clearance to mount the first attack, I would certainly go all-out to hit the NATO airfields. And we must assume that the Warsaw Pact air commanders appreciate the importance of what we call offensive counter-air operations: attacking our airfields, our surface-to-air missile sites and our fighter control and reporting systems – indeed, the whole of our air defence infrastructure.

In the early hours of a war I would have to give top priority to air defence, because unless we could limit the damage to our own airfields and air defence system on the first day of the war, it would become increasingly difficult to mount effective counter-attacks against the enemy airfields and provide air support for our land forces. If the enemy were successful in closing or seriously damaging most of my main airfields in the early hours of the war, he would be well on the way to gaining air superiority. We would have to prevent that.

So on Day 1 of any war we would have to concentrate heavily on air defence. We would have to engage enemy aircraft aggressively from the moment they crossed the inner-German border, with the aim of breaking up their attacks and inflicting high attrition, and thereby minimizing the damage they could cause to our airfields and air defence infrastructure.'

In bracing itself to receive attacks on its airfields and other vital installations, 2 ATAF would have to expect these to come not only from bombs and rockets, but also from the hideous range of chemical weapons (the modern term for war gases) known to be available to the Soviet forces. All NATO forces are equipped with, and trained in the use of, special clothing to protect them from this form of attack. Nevertheless chemical attacks would severely test the morale and training of those subjected to them, and in the contaminated areas all movement would be slowed greatly.

In order to blunt the initial onslaught, 2 ATAF would need to use as interceptors most if not all its F-4s and F-16s with a dual air defence and ground attack capability, to augment the F-15s and those F-4s and F-16s dedicated only to air defence. Moreover, unless there had been reinforcements of fighter aircraft from the USA, the in-theatre interceptors would probably be joined by so-called 'reinforcement fighters' – a proportion of the offensive support aircraft, such as Tornadoes, armed with air-to-air missiles in addition to their guns and sent to fly combat air patrols close to their bases as an additional line of air defence. The remaining attack aircraft would sit out the initial enemy raids in their hardened shelters, with bombs loaded and crews briefed, ready to take off for targets in enemy territory as soon as political clearance were received:

'It might be prudent to put some of our attack aircraft on combat air patrol to help intercept incoming enemy attacks. All of these aircraft are fitted with cannon and can carry Sidewinder missiles, and so have a useful air-to-air capability. Moreover, aircraft sent aloft for this purpose would probably be safer than if they remained on the ground at their bases. Only the newest Soviet tactical attack aircraft, the Fencer, can hit targets accurately at night or in poor weather. The great majority of the Warsaw Pact tactical aircraft would have to come by day and in good weather, if they were to do us any real harm. Under those conditions our 'reinforcement fighters' could be very useful.'

From his own experience leading a Phantom squadron in

attacks on airfields during exercises, the 2 ATAF commander knows well the disruption defending fighters can cause to a raiding force on its way to a target. Even if none of the raiders were shot down, they could be forced to jettison their bombs and bolt for home:

'If the raiding force is getting a free ride into the target and the enemy formation leader can maintain the integrity of his formation, if he can concentrate on navigation and acquire the target early, he should be able to put in an accurate attack. If, on the other hand, the defences harass his force all the way to the target – first with surface-to-air missiles, then with air defence fighters, then with 'reinforcement fighters' – it would be a different matter. The formation would probably break up and some of his pilots – who would be flying over unfamiliar enemy territory – could get themselves lost. Other pilots might be forced to cut in afterburner to evade or accelerate away from attackers, and the fuel consumption of a modern jet aircraft in full afterburner is frighteningly high – up to

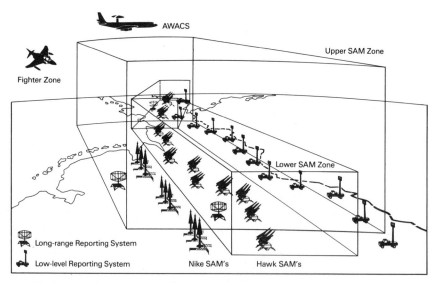

2 ATAF air defence system. Diagrammatic representation, not to scale, showing the volumes of sky in which the low-altitude Hawk surface-to-air missiles and the high-altitude Nike missiles would engage targets. Fighters would engage targets mainly outside these zones

2,000 lb per minute. A pilot cannot afford to use fuel at that rate for long before there will be insufficient to get home if he continues with the mission. Some pilots would probably have to jettison bombs during their attempts to avoid being shot down. If these things happened the defenders would have achieved their main objective, because they would have frustrated the attack – even if none of the aircraft in the raiding force were actually shot down.

I often had attacks disrupted while leading my Phantoms to their targets. It was easy to see what might happen in wartime. If one were bounced by fighters on the way to a target the bombs would cause so much drag that it would be difficult, if not impossible, to evade the attackers. Either one would have to break formation and probably also jettison the bombs, or take the risk and press on for the target. If you kept going, soon afterwards you would probably have somebody in the formation telling you 'Bogey [enemy aircraft] in your 6 o'clock [rear], range 1¼ miles!' And you would then know that you could expect a missile to be launched in your direction at any moment; it would take a very brave man to press on towards the target in a situation like that. If an attack formation is bounced by defending fighters on the way to the target, it usually has a choice: either evade hard and jettison the bombs, or be shot down.'

It is generally accepted that Soviet-trained pilots follow much more rigid tactics than those of Western air forces. How would they cope if their formations were broken up by enemy fighters?

'As with any air force, I suppose much would depend on the quality and initiative of the individual pilot. If his aircraft has a modern navigation/attack system, he ought to be able to get back on track following an engagement and successful evasion, and navigate himself to his target. Now, how good the average Soviet pilot is at looking after himself, as opposed to being looked after by a more experienced leader, I don't know. My hunch is that he would not be as good as his NATO counterpart. Once an attack formation had been broken up it would be hazardous for individual aircraft to continue on to the target – and pilots would know it was hazardous. That is not to say that some of them would not press on and find the target and put down accurate bombs. But there is no doubt in my mind that if our fighters got in amongst the enemy attack formations and scattered them to the four winds, the weight of the attack on our airfields and other vital points would be greatly reduced and far less likely to cause serious damage.'

In parrying any attack by Warsaw Pact aircraft on NATO airfields or other targets, the recently introduced force of E-3 AWACS aircraft would play a major role. The information from AWACS would be integrated with that from the chain of ground radars, to provide air defence fighter controllers with a continual flow of information on the movements of enemy and friendly aircraft:

'AWACS has made a tremendous difference to our air defence capability. Conventional ground radars are able to see low-flying aircraft only when they get comparatively close, within about 30 miles. On the other hand, an AWACS aircraft at 25,000 feet can see low-flying aircraft out to 250 nautical miles, and higher flyers at even greater ranges. It would be able to see Warsaw Pact aircraft as they took off from airfields in East Germany; or, if they came from bases in Poland or the western USSR and approached at low altitude, it would still see them long before they reached NATO territory. The AWACS radar picture can be passed by radio data link to the fighter control centres on the ground, enabling ground controllers to use it to direct our fighters onto incoming raids and pass early warning information to our surface-to-air missile batteries. If key ground control centres were destroyed by enemy action, the AWACS aircraft would be able to take control of our fighters and either broadcast information on the raids or provide specific direction of individual interceptors.

AWACS has greatly improved our ability to get fighters into the right piece of sky at the right time to effect interceptions. It is difficult to put an exact figure to the resultant increase in the effectiveness of our defences against low-flying aircraft, but it could be as high as 300 per cent.'

In time of war AWACS aircraft would almost certainly be
prime targets for the enemy. If they were attacked, could these
large aircraft survive?

'Obviously, no air commander would risk his AWACS aircraft unnecessarily by putting them hard against the inner
German border where they could easily be engaged by enemy
surface-to-air missiles or fighters. We would have to be careful
how we used them. But I am confident that if they remained
behind our surface-to-air missile belts, AWACS aircraft
would not be easy targets for the enemy. However, their crews
would have to be continually on the look-out for enemy
fighters like Foxbat coming after them at high speed and high
altitude. The AWACS aircraft should be able to detect such
an attack in good time; and by diving away to the west at
maximum speed it would extend the chase and draw the
Foxbat to a lower altitude where our fighters and missiles
would have a better chance of engaging it.'

NATO's surface-to-air missile defences in Central Europe are
deployed in layers, which attacking enemy aircraft would have to
penetrate before they could reach targets further back. In the
battle area and immediately behind it, protecting troop concentrations and important targets, would be large numbers of highly
mobile short-range surface-to-air missile systems like Rapier and
Chaperral, and several different types of infantry shoulder-
launched missile. Behind these, some way back from the border,
is a chain of Hawk missile batteries to engage aircraft flying at
low and medium altitudes. Further back still is a belt of Nike
missile batteries to engage enemy aircraft penetrating at medium
or high altitude. As a final line of defence, important targets
such as airfields are ringed with short-range missile or gun
defences.

Because of the danger of 'fratricide' – shooting down one's
own aircraft – unless there were good air-to-ground communications it would be important to separate the operations of
surface-to-air missiles and fighters. In any conflict in Central
Europe, where vast numbers of aircraft would be employed by
both sides, the lack of a reliable system of positive identification

could give rise to severe problems. When large numbers of friendly aircraft were present in a confined area and all radiated IFF (Identification Friend or Foe) replies, there could be times when the identification system was swamped by the volume of incoming signals. And when that happened correct identification replies would not be recognized:

'If we had a really reliable and secure means of electronic identification, then we could operate fighters and engage enemy aircraft with surface-to-air missiles in the same air-space even if our communications had been disrupted. But at present we cannot place 100 per cent reliance on our electronic IFF equipment in a war situation, where there might be thousands of aircraft going backwards and forwards across the battle area. Neither side yet has this capability.'

As soon as political clearance was received for aircraft to attack targets in enemy territory, *offensive* counter-air operations would begin.

'With the numerical imbalance between the NATO and Warsaw Pact Air Forces in the Central Region, we could not expect to gain air superiority by remaining on the defensive. Following the initial attacks by the enemy, we would go onto the offensive ourselves by hitting his airfields hard. The aim would be to reduce the number of sorties the enemy could mount against our airfields and our ground forces. In that way we would hope to throw the enemy air forces off balance and wrest the initiative from them. So that would be our broad philosophy: first to absorb the initial intensive enemy attacks, then as soon as we could to go out and hit his airfields and pin down his aircraft.

If we were able to close some of their most important airfields, for example those operating Fencers or Floggers, let us say for only twelve hours, then during that time none of the aircraft at those bases would be able to fly against us even though they were fully serviceable sitting in their concrete shelters. Several hundred aircraft could be bottled up in that way. Of course, those enemy aircraft that were airborne when our attacks went in could be diverted to other airfields. But if we could force the enemy to use dispersed operating bases where there were no hardened shelters, the aircraft would have to be parked in the open where they would become lucrative targets in their own right. There is no doubt in my mind that if we could successfully block the runways and taxiways at his main offensive operating bases, and keep them blocked with repeat attacks, then we would be well on the way to gaining a favourable air situation.'

The more important Warsaw Pact military airfields facing 2 ATAF are all situated well back in East Germany or Poland; and in front of them in time of war would be the full range of static and mobile surface-to-air missiles, with rings of short-range air defence weapons around the airfields themselves. For an attacking force to stand a good chance of hitting such a target without itself suffering heavy losses, the operation would have to be carefully planned and have support from specialized aircraft:

'We are now going for combined package formations made up of different types of aircraft for attack, escort, reconnaissance, defence suppression and electronic countermeasures, as the best way of penetrating the more densely defended areas. The Americans used 'force packages', as they were known, quite extensively during their air raids into North Vietnam, but their aircraft flew at medium altitude. A modern package formation would go in either at low altitude or medium altitude, depending on the circumstances. During exercises we have practised bringing together forces with as many as twenty-five or thirty aircraft, including EF-111 electronic countermeasures and F-4 defence suppression aircraft. Sometimes the force package might have to fight its way right through to a well-defended target; at other times it might be sufficient to clear a corridor through the enemy's forward surface-to-air defences.

To put a particularly important airfield out of action for twelve hours or more, my planning staff might decide that the attack force required was twelve Tornadoes. Typically, eight of the Tornadoes might be armed with JP233 airfield denial weapons to crater the runways and taxiways, with the other four aircraft carrying conventional free-fall or parachute-retarded bombs to attack the fuel and bomb storage areas and other vital installations. Supporting this force might be two EF-111 jamming escort aircraft, a flight of four F-4 'Wild Weasel' defence suppression aircraft and perhaps six F-15 escort fighters. The package might also include one or two reconnaissance aircraft, for example Jaguars, to take post-strike photos because we would need to know if the attack had been successful. So a typical force package might comprise about twenty-five aircraft of five different types.'

On the way to and from the target the aircraft in the package would fly close enough for crews to maintain visual or radar contact with each other, but not so close that aircraft would get in each other's way. Each aircraft would carry self-protection electronic countermeasures equipment to jam or spoof the radars of enemy surface-to-air missile or gun batteries, or fighters, trying to engage it.

On arrival in the target area the package formation would split into its component units, each with a carefully scripted role. The success of the attack would depend on meticulously accurate navigation and timing by the crews involved. Escorting F-15s would seek to ward off any enemy fighters which might attempt to interfere with the operation. Defence suppression F-4s would attack surface-to-air missile sites protecting the approach to the target and the EF-111s would jam selected radars and attempt to cause maximum confusion amongst the defenders. The Tornadoes would toss conventional free-fall bombs towards the airfield from pull-up points several miles away, or drop parachute-retarded bombs on their targets. The other Tornadoes carrying specialized airfield denial weapons would aim for set points on the runway and taxiways, disgorging scores of bomblets to punch lines of holes across the concrete surfaces, and large numbers of sensitive mines to delay repair work. Finally, the Jaguar reconnaissance aircraft would run past the airfield to photograph the results. Aircraft entering the target area would fly at high speed and low altitude, making full use of ground cover to shield themselves from the defences. From start to finish this well-co-ordinated operation could take less than two minutes, from the time the first Tornado began pulling up to toss its bombs to the time the last reconnaissance Jaguar left the target. Once clear of the target the force package would reform, then head for home:

> 'Soon after our aircraft had departed, the enemy base commander would send in teams to inspect the damage and try to get the airfield back into use as soon as possible. So we would probably need to launch repeated attacks to keep the enemy airfields inoperative. With Tornadoes and F-111s we are able to attack by night or day in virtually any weather, and with great accuracy. If, in the course of follow-up attacks, our aircraft caught enemy repair teams and their specialist plant out in the open, and put them out of action also, then the enemy base commander would have a really serious problem on his hands.'

A co-ordinated attack of this nature, using several different types of aircraft from different units, is probably the most difficult type of air operation to mount. For it to be successful the aircrew need a high standard of training and during the planning stage there has to be scrupulous attention to detail:

> 'Package formations are not easy to bring together or manage in the air, and the crews require specialized training and continual practice. With several different types of aircraft taking part, there may be three or four stations involved in a force package operation, and much advanced planning has to be done if it is to be mounted successfully. But the operating procedures can be developed in peacetime, based on experience during exercises in very realistic training environments, like Red Flag in the USA and Maple Flag in Canada. From those we have a good idea which tactics are likely to work and which are not.'

A penetration deep into enemy territory, then an attack on a heavily defended target followed by a fighting withdrawal, might mean the attacking force having to spend as long as forty minutes over enemy territory exposed to the fighter and surface-to-air defences. Would the likely results from such an attack be worth the loss of two or perhaps more of the participating aircraft?

'With forty Fencers on one airfield, if we did nothing about it, that base could mount at least 100 sorties per day against us. Now, if we were able to close that airfield for twelve to twenty-four hours for the loss of two Tornadoes, that kind of trade-off would be worthwhile. But then I do not accept that we would necessarily suffer such a high rate of attrition in carrying out that kind of operation.

You have to look at the actual attrition rates inflicted on offensive air forces in wars over the past seventy years, compared with the attrition rates which operational analysts had forecast would arise. There has almost invariably been a very big disparity between the two, with aircraft losses in war being much lower than anticipated. There are so many intangible factors which come into play such as surprise, fear, excitement and the fog of war, which are difficult to crunch into a computer when assessing the likely success rate of an anti-aircraft weapons system.

Operational analysts will sometimes forecast that we are likely to suffer 10, 15, or even 20 per cent attrition rates attacking heavily defended targets, attrition rates that would be totally unsustainable; but, except for very short periods of time or during very special operations, such loss rates have never been experienced in war. For example, if one examines the Yom Kippur war in the Middle East in 1973, the Israelis did lose several aircraft over the Golan Heights and the Suez Canal in the first two days of fighting; but at no time did their loss rate rise above 4 per cent. At the time the media were suggesting that manned aircraft could no longer survive in the face of such dense surface-to-air missile and gun defences; and yet by the end of the war the Israeli Air Force had actually flown more than 11,000 sorties over an 18-day period for the loss of 115 aircraft or a rate of just over 1 per cent.

I believe that attack formations with modern aircraft flying at very low level and high speed, supported by electronic

countermeasures, defence suppression and fighter escort aircraft, using accurate intelligence to route themselves clear of
the most densely defended areas and mounting carefully
co-ordinated attacks, would be able to hit their targets and get
back without suffering unacceptably high loss rates. Our
experience in various realistic exercises supports this judge-
ment.'

There has been talk of using AWACS aircraft to guide
formations of attack aircraft to their targets, by routing them
round enemy defences. Would AWACS aircraft be used in this
way over Central Europe?

'While AWACS could be used for this purpose, its primary
use early in the conflict would be air defence. If there were
spare capacity, AWACS could be used for the airborne
direction of attack aircraft. But once a force package of the size
I have described were under way it would probably be
counter-productive to deviate much from the planned route. If
the force had to make a deep penetration to reach its target,
some aircraft would be operating near to the limit of their
radius of action. So if there were too much evasive routing
some of the aircraft could run out of fuel on their way home.
AWACS is primarily an air defence vehicle, but it could be
useful to our offensive forces by giving warning of the movements of enemy fighter patrols. It would then be up to the
force package leader to decide what action should be taken in
response to that advice. It should never be mandatory for the
package leader to follow instructions from the AWACS aircraft, for that might endanger the integrity of the package
formation and its ability to get to the target and back.'

While the defensive and offensive counter-air battles were
getting into their stride, a series of quite separate air operations
would be in progress in direct support of the land battle. These
all come under the heading of offensive air support operations, a
generic term which embraces tactical reconnaissance, battlefield
air interdiction and close air support missions.

Tactical reconnaissance is vitally important to the land force commander, for it is his most reliable means of discovering what is happening in enemy territory beyond the view of his forward observation posts:

'My tactical reconnaissance Phantoms, Jaguars, Mirages, F-16s, Alphajets and Harriers, together with other visual and electronic sensors, would provide an accurate running plot of the disposition and movement of enemy ground forces. Certainly in war we would not rely on satellites, alone, for this information; we could not be sure how long they would survive, and bad weather can greatly reduce the value of satellite photography. So the provision of intelligence is multi-faceted with several systems, especially manned reconnaissance aircraft and drones, providing information on enemy movements.'

For all the exotic modern sensors that are now available, however, it is interesting to note that the oldest aerial reconnaissance sensor of all – the human eye – still has an important part to play:

'Our reconnaissance pilots are all trained in visual reconnaissance, and they would be able to recognize the types of enemy tanks and vehicles they saw moving along a road. As soon as possible after a sighting the pilot would pass the information back by radio and it could be available to army commanders within minutes. Those radio reports would be vitally important. Army commanders want the best and latest reports they can get of what is happening in areas beyond the view of their own reconnaissance systems. Reconnaissance photographs provide useful back-up information, but for the aircraft to return to base, their pilots to be debriefed, film to be developed and interpreted and the information disseminated could take a couple of hours. That might be too long for the army, because in that time an enemy division advancing towards the battle area could move 20 kilometres or more. It is absolutely vital to a corps commander to know the disposition of enemy forces moving forward towards him in the area some 30 to 80 kilometres behind the battle. He cannot move a large ground formation like a brigade or a division into the correct defensive blocking position unless he has advance warning of where the enemy is going and in what force. He needs to be able to plan his defence to counter enemy moves in advance; he certainly does not want to find that suddenly there are two fresh enemy divisions entering the battle and his only reserves are 50 kilometres away. So it is utterly critical that the land force commander is given regular, accurate and timely intelligence on enemy dispositions.

Another very important aspect of intelligence that my tactical aircraft would have to provide is post-attack reconnaissance. Whenever airfields or bridges were attacked, I would need to know quickly how successful the attack had been; and if things had not gone well and we had not hit the targets as planned, we would have to go back and attack them again. Such reconnaissance missions would have to be re-flown at frequent intervals, because I would need to know if the enemy repair teams had worked faster than expected and brought an airfield back into use, or thrown pontoons across a river to replace a bridge that had been destroyed. In such cases the targets would have to be re-attacked. To use my force to best effect I would need the best intelligence I could get.'

Once enemy troops had been detected moving up from their rear areas, short-range attack aircraft would begin flying interdiction missions: attacks on enemy units moving forward in long columns that would be particularly vulnerable to attack from the air, in the zone 10 to 100 kilometres behind the battle area:

'The current Soviet Army attack doctrine is based on the use of forces massed in depth. In any advance westwards they would expect their leading elements to suffer heavy losses, so it would be important to feed fresh units into the battle to sustain the momentum of their advance. Hence the heavy emphasis NATO places on being able to interdict – to cut off – these forces from the battle area.

To reduce the flow of reinforcements significantly we would have to select our targets very carefully. We would try to disrupt their movements by focusing attacks on choke points along the main line of advance – for example, a defile through a line of hills where vehicles might be confined to a single road or a key bridge. By disrupting their advance in this way we would hope to cause huge traffic jams, with vehicles bunched together in the open where they would be highly vulnerable to air attack. Once such a lucrative target had been identified we would task scores of attack aircraft – Harriers, Alphajets, Mirages and NF-5s – to attack it with bombs, rockets and cannon shells.

That should be an extremely effective way to use attack aircraft. The ability to concentrate fire power against the enemy in that way – rapidly, over long distances and with devastating effect – is unique to the air weapon; neither land nor seaborne weapons systems can do that. And within a few hours those same aircraft could be airborne again and concentrating over another target 100 kilometres or more from the first.'

The term 'close air support' is often loosely used, but in the military lexicon it is specifically defined: *air action against hostile targets which are in close proximity to friendly forces, and which require detailed integration of each air mission with the fire and movement of those forces.* By definition this type of mission takes place over or near the land battle, and above the fighting there would be a billowing cloud of dust and smoke cutting visibility close to the ground. The targets, usually enemy tanks, vehicles and artillery, would be spread out over a large area and well camouflaged; the pilot of a high-speed aircraft would have difficulty in seeing them in time to attack accurately on his first pass – and if he went back for a second pass his chances of being shot down by ground fire would increase greatly. Only rarely would vehicles be forced to concentrate in the open in the battle area, to present aircraft with a lucrative target. The proximity of friendly troops compounds the problem: at high speed it is virtually impossible to distinguish a camouflaged friendly tank from a camouflaged enemy tank and there is the ever-present risk that the air attacks might fall on the very troops they were supposed to assist. It was for these reasons that the US Air Force developed a highly specialized aircraft, the A-10, specifically for the close support mission. All aircraft entering the battle area on close air support missions have to be directed on to targets by forward air control officers on the ground or in helicopters, sometimes using laser designators or coloured smoke to mark the enemy positions.

Because of these problems, high-speed aircraft would fly close air support missions only in specific instances where the army commander could not contain the situation with his own infantry, artillery, battlefield helicopters and armoured units:

'Close air support is not an easy operation to mount using high-speed, fixed-wing aircraft. It has to be co-ordinated very closely with what the army are doing: it may be an hour between a request for a close air support mission and the aircraft arriving in the area to mount the attack and in the meantime the ground situation could have changed. So using high-speed aircraft to make that kind of attack is not the most cost-effective way of helping the ground forces. If the army can deal with the problem with their own artillery, tanks, anti-tank missiles and helicopters, then they should; and they recognize that. Commanders in the forward area should not be calling for close air support attacks as an extension of their artillery; that is a misuse of air power. Army commanders agree that, by and large, our fixed-wing aircraft should concentrate on interdiction missions against enemy forces beyond the range of army weapons, where our aircraft can be so much more effective than in the immediate battle area.

We would send high-speed aircraft to mount close air support missions only if things were going badly for our ground forces. For example, if our forces had been caught off balance and had insufficient time to get into their main defensive positions when Warsaw Pact forces came over the border, then we would have to mount concentrated air attacks to slow the enemy advance and buy time for our troops to complete their deployment. We saw an example of this in the Arab–Israeli conflict in 1973, the Yom Kippur War, when the Syrian Army launched a surprise attack and their tanks were pouring through the defences on the Golan Heights, just a few miles from the point where they could drop down on to the

Israeli plains. But they were held up for more than a day by
concentrated air attacks, and this gave the Israeli Army time
to consolidate its main defensive positions. It was a classic
example of the use of aerial fire power, concentrated in space
and time and very rapidly, to buy time for the ground forces to
seal off an enemy breakthrough.

Other occasions when we could provide really effective
close air support would be during a counter-attack by our
forces, when maximum possible fire power would be required
to punch through before the enemy could bring up reserves; or
if our forces had created a 'killing zone', a salient into which a
large number of enemy tanks and other vehicles had been
drawn and could usefully be attacked by fixed-wing aircraft.

But apart from specific situations like those I have described, our high-speed attack aircraft are likely to provide the
greatest help to the land commander by going a bit deeper
into enemy territory and attacking forces moving towards the
battle but beyond the range of army weapons. For unless the
air forces do something about them those enemy units would
come fresh into the battle, unmolested and well organized,
twenty-four or thirty-six hours later.'

In the Commander's view, the best types of aircraft to deal
with enemy tanks in the immediate battle area are the A-10s and
small helicopters like the Lynx, Cobra or BO 105 using anti-tank
guided missiles:

'Army helicopters armed with missiles would, I believe, be
very effective against tanks in the forward area, particularly if
the helicopters operated in areas clear of enemy anti-aircraft
weapons. By making maximum use of ground cover and lying
in ambush, popping up above the treeline only to fire their
missiles, these helicopters could exact a heavy toll on enemy
tanks. I see armed helicopters as complementary to fixed-wing
aircraft, rather than in competition with them. One does not
buy an expensive aircraft like the Harrier to kill tanks one at a
time in the forward area, except in an emergency. The
Harrier's main role is to hit the enemy ground forces further
back where they are not deployed for battle and thus present

more concentrated targets, and where our relatively low-speed helicopters would be vulnerable to enemy air defence weapons and small arms fire.'

A fairly recent addition to the Soviet inventory has been the Hind gunship, a heavily armed and armoured helicopter with an all-up weight about twice that of the Lynx. The Hind has been described as a 'helicopter battle-cruiser'; in time of war it would operate offensively in large numbers over the battle area and enemy-held territory, serving as a tank-killer in its own right but also able to land squads of troops behind the enemy lines. Is there a place for such a large, multi-purpose battlefield helicopter in NATO's order of battle?

'Personally I am not persuaded that we should invest heavily in heavily armoured helicopters that could operate deep into enemy territory. I believe the Soviets have put too much faith in the helicopter gunship. In saying this, I do not mean to imply that they could not inflict considerable damage to NATO forces with attack helicopters like the Hind; my reservations centre mainly on their vulnerability. Even using modern sensors the crews of attack helicopters will have difficulty locating our troops and armour lying in wait in defensive positions, and flying relatively slowly close to the ground they would inevitably expose themselves to engagement by many types of weapon – Rapier and infantry shoulder-launched surface-to-air missiles, tank and small arms fire. The evidence from the conflicts in Vietnam, the Middle East and Afghanistan indicates to me that Soviet attack helicopters would suffer heavy losses if they attempted to bring their fire power to bear against NATO forces in well-prepared defensive positions. Soviet forces have lost well over 300 helicopters in Afghanistan over the last five years. We are told that Soviet helicopters like Hip and Hind would be used for airborne assault operations, landing troops behind our lines and for *coup de main* operations to seize key bridges and other important objectives. Well, that sort of operation could be very risky and costly, although I accept that it could come off from time to time. We would have to watch out very carefully for any forward deployment of attack and assault helicopters from their main airfields in East Germany to forward operating locations near the border. We have the sensors to identify their movements, and our attack aircraft could hit these helicopters and their support facilities on the ground. Once the helicopters were airborne and operating in the forward area, I believe they would best be engaged by army gun and missile systems. The NATO ground forces have a wide range of weapons that would be effective against low-flying helicopters.

All that said, I am not playing down this element of the threat. The Warsaw Pact forces have a very large number of attack and transport helicopters and they could do us a lot of harm by sheer weight of numbers. But they would undoubtedly suffer heavy losses in the process.'

Any type of short-range attack aircraft could be sent to engage enemy helicopters operating in large numbers over the battle area, but a particularly potent counter to this threat is the German Air Force Alphajet; 2 ATAF has two squadrons of these aircraft, which can be fitted with 27 mm cannon with which to engage helicopters. Although strictly subsonic, the Alphajet is quite fast enough for this task and its extremely high manoevrability would make it very effective in this role.

Having gone into some detail on how 2 ATAF would operate in time of war, Air Marshal Hine outlined some of the ways in which he and his staff would seek to control the air battle:

'Having started the conflict using well-prepared tactical plans for the conduct of the initial air operations, my battle staff and I would need to monitor closely the progress of operations from several viewpoints. For example: how successful were our attacks against enemy airfields? Were we doing enough damage to put them out of action and keep them inoperative? Were we greatly reducing the number of offensive sorties by the enemy air force, and if we were not why not? Were our loss rates high, and if so why? Were our tactics and operating procedures sound? And could we improve our electronic warfare and defence suppression techniques? These would be some of the crucial questions to which I would constantly seek answers.

At the same time we would be keeping a close eye on the level of damage being inflicted on our airfields, air defence and other key target systems, and deciding what measures could be taken to reduce it. And we would be doing everything possible to repair damage and replace losses.

At least twice a day I would meet the Commander of NATO's Northern Army Group to review the progress of the land–air battle and discuss the allocation of offensive air support effort to the various army corps. If, for example, major enemy thrusts were coming into the British and the Netherlands corps areas, then our offensive air support effort would be allotted accordingly. But if the battle suddenly took an unexpected turn and a serious threat developed in the Belgian corps area, then offensive air support could be switched there at short notice. In any major conflict in Central Europe there would be no separate land and air battles. We could only hope to succeed by fighting a joint land–air battle from the outset.'

During the management of air operations it would be necessary for aircraft engaged in some roles to fly sorties at their maximum possible rate, while others might be held on the ground until there was an opportunity to use them effectively:

'In the case of air defence, we would have to make sure that we did not commit too many of our fighters at any one time. It would be all too easy to scramble everything we have to meet the initial enemy raids; and then, at precisely the moment when our fighters landed to refuel and re-arm, the enemy might mount even heavier attacks and we would have little or nothing with which to meet them except for the surface-to-air missiles. So we would have to husband our air defence fighters very carefully.

As far as offensive operations are concerned, the first two days of the battle would be crucial if we were to create a favourable air situation for our land and air forces. So during that period I would see myself committing most of my aircraft capable of offensive counter-air operations, at maximum sortie rates, to the vital task of pinning down the enemy air forces on their airfields.

With the short-range attack aircraft suitable only for offensive air support operations, on the other hand, I would want to withhold them until we had identified potentially lucrative targets for them to attack. When we did, I would send in a large number of aircraft to launch a series of concentrated attacks to create as much destruction, disruption and delay as possible. Until further suitable targets were identified, these aircraft would be held on standby on the ground in their protective shelters. I would certainly not want to fritter away my attack aircraft in penny packets on, say, search-and-destroy missions over enemy territory or providing close air support for our land forces when no critical situation existed. Those types of operation would be unlikely to inflict much damage on the enemy, and cumulatively they could lose us quite a lot of aircraft.'

We have looked at the possible course of a conventional war in the air over Central Europe. But how likely is that scenario ever to be enacted? And if it were, how long could fighting continue before one side or the other was forced to use nuclear weapons?

'Historically the Soviets have shown they are a cautious people. They will of course continue to exploit any situation where they believe there is no real risk of a confrontation with the USA, but as long as the USA remains firmly committed to Western European defence, I think the chances of a pre-planned major war in Europe are very remote. We have, however, got to maintain a credible deterrent in the eyes of the Soviet Union. If there were to be a significant weakening of the strong American commitment of forces to Europe, i.e. an isolationist policy, or a breakdown of political cohesion in Western Europe through the collapse of one or two democratically elected governments, a situation might just arise where a hawkish Soviet leadership could think it worthwhile to nibble at pieces of NATO territory. But so long as NATO remains militarily strong and politically stable until meaningful disarmament agreements can be made, I think that is very unlikely.

If we ever did get locked into an all-out conventional war in Central Europe, most likely through a miscalculation, it is very difficult to forecast how long that would last before we might have to resort to the use of nuclear weapons. I do not see how an all-out conventional war could last much beyond three or four weeks. The consumption of weapons would be enormous – in a single day a squadron of Tornadoes could put down 80 tons of bombs, a squadron of air defence F-15s could get through 180 air-to-air missiles. No Western nation can afford the money to provide for the expenditure of bombs and missiles at such a rate for very long.

Given the numerical imbalance between the two sides, if our forces were in danger of imminent defeat and there were no sign of a return to the negotiating table, we would be faced with the awful decision of having to use nuclear weapons or accept the collapse of our conventional defences. And if the nuclear threshold were to be crossed, how would these weapons first be used? One option would be to set off a few low-yield tactical nuclear weapons on military targets to demonstrate our political resolve. What that would amount to in terms of actual weapons put down, I don't know; it might be two, six, twelve, it might even be twenty. The intention would be to say to the other side: 'Look, if you carry on like this, we could find ourselves getting into all-out nuclear exchange with massive losses on both sides.' And then, hopefully, the enemy would decide that we meant business and return to the negotiating table. Another option, if our conventional defences started to collapse and the decision had been taken to use nuclear weapons first, would be to seek to restore the military situation. That could involve the use of many more tactical nuclear weapons. The danger of the first option, as I see it, is that if we were to use just a few nuclear weapons to demonstrate our resolve, the enemy might say, 'To Hell with you!' and reply with a massive tactical nuclear strike in response to our very modest initial use of these weapons. Then, of course, we would be even worse off militarily and be faced with the prospect of having to escalate to the use of strategic nuclear weapons.

Once either side resorts to nuclear weapons, it is impossible to say where this could lead. That is why it is vitally important to maintain the nuclear threshold as high as we can. And that is why we have got to maintain a high level of expenditure on conventional forces as part of our posture of deterrence, certainly until such time as balanced and verifiable disarmament arrangements can be agreed between NATO and the Warsaw Pact.

2: Integrating the Land–Air Battle, a Soldier's View

Colonel Keith Robson joined the British Army in 1958 and was commissioned into the Royal Artillery. In 1964 he began training as a helicopter pilot and flew as an artillery observation pilot in Aden. In 1972 he took command of No. 657 Squadron, operating Sioux and later Gazelle reconnaissance helicopters with the 7th Armoured Brigade in Germany. In 1975 he returned to England and was posted to Headquarters Army Air Corps at Middle Wallop, in charge of operations and organization. In 1978 he took command of a regiment operating two, later three, helicopter squadrons as part of the 4th Armoured Division in Germany. In 1981 he joined the staff at Headquarters Northern Army Group in Germany where he was one of those responsible for co-ordinating air and land operations. At the end of 1984 he was promoted to Colonel and took up a staff appointment at Army Air Corps headquarters. In this chapter he discusses some of the ways in which the Air Force might be expected to assist the Army in fighting the land battle.

'At Headquarters Northern Army Group I was the Lieutenant-Colonel Chief G3 Air, the army link man for land–air operations on the staff of Commander Northern Army Group but working jointly with the Commander 2 ATAF. In peacetime the joint Army/Air Force headquarters is situated at Rheindahlen near Mönchen-Gladbach in Germany. The Land Commander's and the Air Commander's offices are no more than ten yards apart and there is a joint Air Force/Army Secretariat. All the planning is done jointly, and neither service can write a plan without the other knowing what it is doing. In time of war the two headquarters might split and deploy to other locations, but the two staffs would work together closely in planning their operations.'

Senior NATO army commanders accept that the air force would probably be giving the most help to their troops when it was hitting targets many miles or tens of miles beyond the battle area:

'The ex-Commander Northern Army Group, General Nigel Bagnall, used to say that his priorities for our air forces were to keep the enemy air force off his back and to stop the enemy's second echelon of reserves from linking up with their front echelon. He would defeat their front echelon, but he needed to prevent the enemy from reinforcing the battle area. And when he wanted to counter-attack, he wanted air superiority and concentrated support in that area while he was attacking. That was what he required from his air commander and he accepted that it could mean that during the initial days of the conflict his troops might not see a single friendly attack aircraft, other than those passing through their area at high speed on their way to and from targets beyond the battle area. He accepted that only when the counter-air battle had been fought successfully, and the enemy air forces contained, could a proportion of the longer-range air force units be released for deep interdiction missions.

The army would have to accept that, because if the battle between the opposing air forces were lost, not only would it get little or no air support when its own battle reached a crucial stage, but its troops would be unable to move without being battered by the enemy air force. So, during the initial stage of the battle, it would be no good the army saying 'Our priority is for deep interdiction missions to hit marshalling yards', if nearly all of our aircraft that could do deep interdiction were tied up with offensive counter-air missions against enemy airfields.'

In time of war, after the requirements of the offensive counter-air battle had been met, Keith Robson and staff officers working with him would have been responsible for allocating the attack aircraft available to support the army, the so-called 'air alloc':

'With three others, I would work out the air alloc each day. The Assistant Chief of Staff Offensive Operations, an RAF group captain, would announce the number of aircraft available for offensive air support operations. Whatever the state of the counter-air battle during its initial stages, we in the Army would always have allocated to us most of the shorter-range attack aircraft like the Alphajets, A-10s and Harriers which cannot go deep into enemy territory to attack airfields. They would be available for offensive air support.'

Once the army commander knew how many aircraft he had been allocated for offensive air support, his planning staff would assign them to the corps commanders and to interdiction targets in order of priority. Almost always there would be far more requests for air attacks than aircraft able to carry them out.

As soon as he had long-range attack aircraft assigned to him, the army commander would want to begin deep interdiction attacks against targets more than 100 km (about 60 miles) behind the battle area. The transport system carrying enemy reinforcing units on their way to the battle area would be amongst the high-priority targets marked down for destruction:

'I would expect our air force to attack the road, rail and bridge network in the enemy rear area during the early stages of a war. That would be a high-priority target.

Take a map of East Germany and look at the area from the Baltic south to Berlin and beyond. See how much water there is – lakes, rivers and canals. It is not a big, wide open prairie which an army can drive across without restriction. There are definite areas through which tanks and other heavy vehicles could not possibly go.

Now think of the number of troops and vehicles in a Warsaw Pact second echelon army: about 150,000 men and 40,000 vehicles. And there might be three such armies to move forward. Even if we did nothing at all to interfere with their movement, it would be a colossal problem to move such a large force up to the battle area.

So if Warsaw Pact forces were to move west in anything like their full strength they would have to take certain routes and they could have very real problems. Using our air force to disrupt the flow of their tremendous mass of equipment towards the west would be a most effective way to slow their advance. Air attacks would never be able to stop enemy movement completely, but they could cause enormous chaos.'

Bridges are not easy targets for air attack, however. They are relatively small, difficult to knock down and usually well defended. In the 2 ATAF inventory the most effective weapon against them is the laser-guided bomb, released from aircraft like the F-111F (see Chapter 5). To cause the greatest possible disruption to enemy movement, such attacks would have to be carefully timed:

'The nicety of bridge dropping is to time it to cause maximum disruption to the enemy troops moving forward. If, for example, we thought that part of the enemy follow-up force was going to cross a river the following night, it would not be a good idea to knock down the bridge they might use at 6 a.m. in the morning. If we did that, it would allow the enemy commander twelve hours in which to make alternative arrangements to cross the river. It would be much more effective if we could drop the bridge just as the leading enemy units were about to cross it. Then their vehicles would probably have to turn round and go back some way, before moving to one side to cross the river at another point. That could be difficult if the road were jammed with vehicles.

It is a bit like travelling along a motorway listening to the traffic report on the radio, and hearing that there had been a major accident ahead. If you knew well in advance you could look at your road map, work out an alternative route to bypass the obstruction and continue on with little delay. But if you discovered the blocked road only when you joined the traffic tail-back, you would be stuck and it might take a long time to resume the journey.'

The shorter-range attack aircraft would be allocated to those corps commanders whom the army commander considered were in greatest need:

'The army commander would decide which parts of his front required the greatest weight of air support, usually those where the major enemy thrusts were developing. An exception would be if one of our corps had been seriously weakened in a previous battle and had run short of ammunition, and was in a poor condition to meet even a relatively weak enemy thrust. In such a case it might be necessary to give that corps most or all of the available air support, to keep it going until it could be resupplied or reinforced. That corps would need air support more than one facing a main enemy thrust but in good shape, fresh and with plenty of ammunition.

About 100 kilometres in front of each corps is the limit of the corps commander's planning responsibility for air operations. The corps commander would task the attack aircraft allocated to him to hit targets he selected in the zone between that line and his forward positions. He would decide whether these aircraft would be best employed in interdiction missions to stop enemy follow-on forces reaching the battle area, or whether the battle had reached a critical phase and it was necessary to use the bulk of his allocation for close air support.'

The greater proportion of the attacks mounted by the shorter-range aircraft would be against enemy ground forces behind the battle area but moving forward:

'If there was a target in that area which the corps commander wanted hit, he would ask his staff to task aircraft to attack it. Typically he might say, 'I have discovered an enemy armoured division in woods in such and such a position, 70 kilometres in front of my forward positions, preparing to reinforce the battle area. I want it stopped.' His air force staff at corps headquarters would pass the target to the ATOC [Air Task Operations Centre], the tasking agency at 2 ATAF, which would order squadrons allocated to the corps to attack the target.

The army could use long-range artillery fire to establish corridors through the enemy air defences to assist forces of attack aircraft on their way to and from targets, in order to suppress the enemy air defences. By putting down heavy barrage fire for a specific period into the sea around, say, an SA-6 anti-aircraft missile battery, our gunners could make the enemy operators keep their heads down. That would be suppressive fire rather than destructive fire; the chances of destroying any of the radars or missile launchers might be low. But if a surface-to-air missile operator was trying to shoot down an aeroplane and suddenly artillery shells started exploding all around him, he would certainly find it distracting.

The problem, always, would be one of finding the positions of the targets accurately enough to engage them. The business of locating targets, not only for our artillery but also for the air force, would be a continuing struggle.'

Drones, small remotely controlled aircraft carrying cameras, would be a useful source of intelligence in the area behind the battlefield. These come under the control of army divisional commanders, although the information they bring back would become part of the overall intelligence picture:

'Drones would be used to look at possible targets short distances behind the FEBA [Forward Edge of the Battle Area]. All corps in the Northern Army Group have drones. From intelligence sources we might detect signs of enemy activity in a certain area, and would send a drone to find out what was happening there. There would not be a constant traffic of drones quartering the battle area looking for potential targets. Division or corps would probably be controlling the drones, but they also report their findings to the Army Group headquarters to assist with the all-sources intelligence picture.'

Once the opposing land forces were in close contact, initially there would be no requirement for large-scale air force involvement over the battle area. Keith Robson stressed that attack from the air is only one of several methods of stopping an enemy armoured thrust, and all such weapons would have to be used to their maximum effect in an all-arms co-ordinated action. Until things started to go wrong, the attack aircraft would be better used to slow the movement of enemy reinforcements and supplies into the battle area:

'I would not expect the army to want direct air force help in the straight slug-it-out battle when ground forces were in close contact with each other. NATO's anti-tank capability has improved greatly in the last ten years with the advent of the new infantry anti-tank missiles like Milan, HOT and TOW, both on helicopters and ground vehicles. Also our new tanks, the Leopard, the Abrams and the Challenger, have a greatly improved anti-tank capability compared with their predecessors. So in a close-in battle the army has many systems for stopping enemy tanks.

When the army would need help from the air force would be if enemy forces were advancing through an area where, for some reason, the army was unable to bring its own anti-tank weapons to bear. For example, there might be a battle in progress between a couple of our brigades and two enemy divisions. It might be going well from our point of view, with our troops holding them and destroying a lot of their tanks. However, an enemy tank unit might have forced its way through the gap between our two brigades, and if it continued another 5 or 10 kilometres it would threaten the rear of our force.

Then the corps commander would need to call upon the air force to stop them, to pin them to the ground to give him time to re-deploy ground anti-tank units – tanks, Milan missile teams – to seal off the breakthrough and restore the situation. That would be just the sort of situation where attack aircraft like Harriers, A-10s, and anti-tank helicopters would need to be brought in. These aircraft would be used not in twos and threes, but in concentrations of two or three dozen. And they would operate in concert with our artillery.'

If they could, the corps planning staff would try to time the

attack to coincide with the arrival of the enemy force at a natural
obstacle such as a defile, a river, or a minefield, which would
cause vehicles to start to bunch:

'Once the enemy force entered the designated area the
artillery would engage first, to get the tanks to close down and
cause as much damage as possible to the air defence systems.
Next the anti-tank helicopters would attack with missiles, to
pick off the anti-aircraft weapons, command tanks and other
key vehicles. At the head of the enemy force might be
mine-clearing tanks fitted with flails or bulldozer blades: key
vehicles in any attempt to breach our minefields; the helicopters would aim to pick off these.

Once the helicopters had stopped the leading elements of
the enemy force, those coming behind would bunch up and
that would create an ideal target for Harriers, A-10s,
Alphajets and the other types of attack aircraft.

In this type of attack each element would set up the
situation for the one that followed: the artillery fire would
force the enemy tank crews to close down, the helicopters
would pick off the air defence weapons and hopefully knock
out the leading tanks to bring the force to a temporary halt.
The result would be concentrations of vehicles in a state of
confusion, ideal targets for the high-speed attack aircraft.
Once it had been set up, such an attack would take place
quickly, with some ten minutes elapsing between the first
artillery round exploding in the target area and the last
Harrier leaving it.'

Aircraft engaged in close air support missions in the vicinity of
friendly troops have to be directed on to their targets by forward
air controllers (FACs) either on the ground or in the air. The
controllers pass the details of the target to the attacking pilots by
radio, and may mark the target with laser or coloured smoke. If
the targets are large, the attacking pilots would have little
difficulty in finding them:

'It would be no use an FAC giving the pilot of a high-speed jet
a target like 'Single camouflaged tank in corner of large brown

field behind bushy-topped tree'. Those days are gone. The sort of target they would now expect aircraft to hit would be 'The village in grid square so-and-so, which is absolutely stiff with enemy armoured vehicles moving into the back of it and coming out the front of it. And none of our troops are in there because they have withdrawn behind the line of a certain road'. That is the sort of information an FAC would now give an attack pilot, who would then know that every cluster of vehicles seen in that village would be enemy and there would be no shortage of targets.'

By imposing delays on an enemy force which had broken through, such attacks would give the defenders time to establish themselves in blocking positions ahead of the advance:

'Artillery, anti-tank helicopters and attack aircraft might be able to halt an enemy advance, but they cannot themselves hold ground. Only ground troops can do that. Once the enemy had been stopped, the ground forces would have to take over.

During Exercise Lionheart, which took place in Germany in 1984, the British Army's 6th Brigade demonstrated its ability to seal off such a breakthrough. This brigade has a large number of Milan anti-tank missile teams and is organized to be air transportable; it could be lifted into blocking positions ahead of an enemy advance by Puma or Chinook helicopters.'

In large-scale actions of the type described, most of the land fighting would take place during the day and most of the movement of troops and supplies would be by night:

'Generally speaking, I would expect the enemy follow-up forces to try to cross rivers at night. That would be common sense because even if the bridges were still up, the vehicles would have to bunch to get over the river. If they crossed in the daytime they would make a good target in a place that would be known to us. Even though modern attack aircraft are more effective by night than ever before, it would still be a lot more dangerous for troops to move by day than by night.

If major units could be prevented from crossing a series of river obstacles by night, it could throw out of gear the enemy commander's timetable and he might decide to accept the risks and send his troops across rivers by day – and that could provide some marvellous targets for our daylight attack squadrons.'

The importance of imposing delays on the movement of enemy reinforcing units westwards would be crucial to the management of the land battle in Central Europe. That, with reconnaissance and the prevention of enemy air attacks on its troops, are the main ways in which the air force would be expected to assist the army in the land battle:

'The army would want the air force to prevent or delay enemy follow-on forces moving forward to join those at the front. If the air force could do that, the land commander would be able to take on the enemy's leading elements and even launch counter-attacks to re-take lost ground. But he could do that only so long as those powerful enemy follow-on forces could be kept out of the battle. That would be one of the main things the army would look to the air force to provide. The other is for the air force to win the counter-air battle, because if the enemy air attack operations were not curtailed they could cause major problems to our forces when they were redeploying and mounting counter-attacks. Just as our attack aircraft could cause chaos to enemy forces moving in the open, their attack aircraft could cause similar chaos to us.'

3: The Air Defence Battle

Major Charles 'Chuck' Casey joined the US Air Force in 1969 and after completing pilot training went to Vietnam in 1970 and flew as a forward air controller. In 1971 he returned to the USA and served as a flying instructor, first on T-38s and later on F-5s. In 1978 he was posted to Nellis AFB, Nevada, then to Clark AFB in the Philippines, to an 'Aggressor' unit flying F-5 aircraft to provide air combat training for other fighter pilots. Late in 1981 he converted to the F-15 fighter and in February 1982 he was posted to the 32nd Tactical Fighter Squadron. At the time of the interview he was operations officer of the unit.

The 32nd Fighter Squadron has an establishment of twenty-four McDonnell Douglas F-15C Eagle fighters and is based at Soesterberg near Utrecht in Holland. The F-15C is a large, single-seat twin-engined night and all-weather air superiority fighter, capable of supersonic speed at all altitudes; at take-off in the combat configuration it tips the scales at just over twenty-five tons. Although the maker's brochure credits the F-15C with the ability to attack ground targets with cannon, bombs and rockets, the 32nd TFS would not operate in that role and its pilots do not train for it.

At full power with afterburner, the thrust from the F-15's two engines almost equals the weight of the aircraft. This gives the F-15 a sparkling performance in the climb and enables it to sustain high-g turning manoeuvres:

'With earlier fighter types there was a trade-off, the harder you turned the more airspeed you lost. With the F-15 it is different. Its engines develop enough thrust for it to sustain a high-g turn without the airspeed falling away. That is a feature of all the new types of fighter now coming into service, including the Soviet ones. The F-15 is a good dogfighting aircraft at all speeds.'

The F-15C is fitted with the powerful APG-63 radar, an advanced pulse-doppler set able to locate and track aircraft above the radar horizon at ranges in excess of eighty miles, and to see low-flying aircraft at somewhat shorter ranges provided they are flying toward or away from the fighter. Linked to the radar is an air-to-air IFF interrogator system, to trigger the transponders of friendly aircraft within the volume of sky being scanned:

'Flying the F-15 requires a somewhat different attitude to simpler types of fighter. The pilot has to be something of a systems manager. The F-15 carries a lot of electronic gadgetry which gives a great deal of useful information, but not all of that information will be necessary to the pilot at the time he gets it. An inexperienced pilot flying an F-15 can easily become overloaded with information. But once a pilot becomes used to the airplane, which does not take very long, it is a very effective fighter.'

Normally the F-15C carries an armament of four AIM-7F Sparrow radar semi-active missiles, four AIM-9L Sidewinder infra-red homing missiles and an internally fitted fast-firing 20 mm cannon. This diverse armament gives the F-15 a formidable air-to-air fighting capability. The AIM-7F Sparrow is the fighter's primary weapon for beyond-visual-range (BVR) engagements and is at its most effective when fired at enemy aircraft approaching head-on. The missile homes on signals from the APG-63 radar bounced off the target, which means that the radar has to be locked on to the target from a time before the missile is launched until it reaches the target – and that could take more than a minute. While the F-15's radar is locked on to one target the F-15 pilot cannot engage another aircraft with Sparrow, because he must have continual radar illumination of the target he is engaging. And while his radar is locked on to a target he cannot use it to observe other aircraft in the area. The maker's brochure credits the AIM-7F Sparrow with an engagement range in excess of forty miles. Over Central Europe the missile would be at its most effective during the initial hours of a conflict, when all aircraft crossing the frontier would be hostile and the NATO fighters could engage them at long range. Under such conditions these missiles could do great execution amongst incoming attack formations.

Once the main air battle had been joined, however, there could be many hundreds of aircraft from both sides crossing the battle area at any one time. Then there would be far fewer opportunities for long-range engagements with air-to-air missiles. The big problem is that of differentiating between the blip from a hostile aircraft on a radar screen and that from a friendly one. As mentioned earlier, when large numbers of friendly aircraft are present and all radiate IFF replies, there may be times when the identification system will be swamped and correct reply signals will not be recognized. It is essential to identify targets as hostile before engaging them, and in a confused tactical situation it would often be difficult to do so with confidence by electronic means. The ability of current weapons systems to destroy aircraft at long range far exceeds the ability of current identification systems to determine reliably whose side they belong to:

'The Sparrow has a beyond-visual-range engagement capability, but we can't use it beyond visual range unless we have a positive identification that the aircraft we are firing at is hostile. When the main air battle is in progress, with huge numbers of aircraft from both sides going back and forth over northern Germany, we probably could not use our BVR capability. In a situation like that we could not afford to risk shooting down our own people. If there were several aircraft out in front of us swirling around, obviously we would not lob AIM-7s into the centre of that lot unless we could identify our targets with a high degree of confidence. So when we get to the point where our identification features do not allow BVR engagements, we will have to close on targets until we can identify them visually.'

To assist the identification of aircraft within visual range the

F-15 has a simple optical telescope fixed to look forward from behind the windscreen:

> 'In a lot of cases we would need to close to within one or two miles to identify an aircraft visually; it would depend on its aspect and visibility in the area. And of course there are a whole lot of things that can give a clue as to whether an aircraft is one of theirs or one of ours. Obviously if I saw an F-15 with a very small aircraft chasing it, I would want to shoot down that very small aircraft. I wouldn't need to identify it as a MiG-21 or whatever.'

Although Sparrow can be used to engage targets which have been identified visually, like all long-range missiles it accelerates to high speed after launch and this means its minimum engagement range – that inside which it cannot guide itself on to a target – is relatively long. For this reason, the F-15 carries the somewhat slower AIM-9L Sidewinder missile for short-range engagements. The Sidewinder homing head picks up infra-red energy emitted by the target aircraft; the greatest source of this energy is the jet exhaust, though at high speed the airflow will warm an aircraft's structure sufficiently to attract these missiles. The AIM-9L is credited with the ability to engage targets from any aspect, but is at its most effective when fired into the target's rear hemisphere. Once its infra-red head is locked on the target and the Sidewinder is on its way, the missile requires no further assistance. The launching aircraft is then free to engage another target or break away, as its pilot wishes.

For engagements at very short range, below about three-quarters of a mile, the F-15 would use its 20 mm cannon. Prior to the Vietnam War it was felt that the gun had been rendered obsolescent by the air-to-air guided missile, but Chuck Casey has no doubt that it still has an important place in a modern air-superiority fighter.

> 'A gun is essential during a short-range manoeuvring engagement. In South East Asia kills were lost because some of our fighters didn't have guns. When the F-15 was in its development phase the air force was not going to put in a gun

because the airplane's radar and missiles were considered so advanced. Luckily the fighter pilots were able to talk them into retaining it. I think missile technology will have to advance quite a bit before we can dispense with the gun. Obviously, if we could shoot down an aircraft 1,000 feet in front with a missile that would be great; but I don't know of any missile in service or in development that can arm and guide itself on to a target that soon after launch.

Also, having a gun helps when we have to identify targets visually. Otherwise we might have to go in to short range to identify an aircraft, and if it was hostile we would then have to increase the range before we could launch a missile at it. That is another reason why people fought hard for a cannon in the F-15.'

To accommodate the two big engines and the extensive radar and avionics systems, the F-15 had to be a large aircraft. And for good turning performance at all altitudes the F-15 has a wing area of over 600 square feet, larger than that of other combat aircraft in 2 ATAF. In a dogfight the very size of the F-15 could prove an embarrassment, because in a combat the pilot who is the first to see his opponent has the initiative in any action which follows:

'The big problem with the F-15 is its size. It can be seen a long way away. Also, the engines are supposed to be smoke-free but they do smoke a bit. Would I like to change the F-15? Yes, I'd like to make it a lot smaller if I could. But with the systems fitted to the plane there is probably no way they could all go into a smaller one.'

When there is likely to be sufficient warning of the approach of enemy aircraft, F-15s will wait on the ground on QRA (Quick Reaction Alert), perhaps with pilots at readiness in their cock-pits, ready to get airborne at short notice to intercept specific targets. If for any reason there is insufficient warning, or if there is almost continuous enemy air activity, fighters may be scram-bled and sent to waiting areas from which they will be directed to engage targets. Fighters have to engage enemy aircraft where they find them, and most air-to-air engagements over Central Europe would probably take place below 5,000 feet, though there might be a few high-altitude interceptions above 60,000 feet. From a fighter pilot's point of view the easiest type of interception is when he is directed on to his target by a ground or airborne controller. But, in the chaos of war, fighters would more often have to engage enemy aircraft as best they could without such assistance:

'Often we would be controlled on to enemy aircraft by an AWACS aircraft or a GCI [Ground Controlled Interception radar] site. We can take control from either. It does not matter to us where the radar picture comes from so long as we get accurate control. Obviously we prefer close control if we can have it. A fighter pilot wants as much information on the enemy as he can get. The controller would tell me where the enemy aircraft were and what they were doing, without my having to put my head in the cockpit to interpret what was on my radar. With help from a good controller we can nearly always manoeuvre on to the tail of the target aircraft. It reduces the chances of mistakes in radar interpretation and failure to get into an attacking position.

But in a war I could not expect that sort of help to be available at all times. So we train for the worst case, when we might have to fight with minimal GCI assistance or none at all. We have a system which we call 'Bullseye Control', in which the controller gives us the distance and bearing of the enemy aircraft we are to attack relative to a pre-briefed geographical point. Once we reach that area we would have to find targets for ourselves.'

During partially controlled or freelance interception missions over friendly territory, it is important that in the heat of combat fighter pilots do not enter areas defended by 'friendly' surface-to-air missiles or guns without first getting clearance:

'A fighter pilot needs to know the ground in front of him and on each side at all times, but in the heat of battle he might sometimes lose track of his position. I envision that in the excitement of a high-speed chase after enemy aircraft some of our people might allow themselves to be drawn into our missile defended areas. Anybody who did that would put himself in a very hazardous situation, because at some readiness states the missile operators might be cleared to shoot at anything that came within range.'

Modern air-fighting tactics are based on the use of elements of two aircraft with each providing cover for the other. The F-15s would endeavour to engage enemy aircraft in much the same way as did the high-scoring aces of the First World War – run in to attack with the advantage of speed, height and surprise, hit the enemy hard, then get out of range before he can retaliate:

'The normal tactical element in which F-15s operate is the pair. If we wanted to put greater fire power into a given area we could put up four or more aircraft, but they would normally engage in elements of two.

Once I decided to commit myself to the attack I would accelerate to go as fast as I could, Mach 1.2 or 1.4 or even faster. That would get me into an attacking position quicker. And if for some reason I was unable to knock down the enemy aircraft it would give me the speed to get out of the fight quickly, regardless of what the enemy aircraft did. For a fighter pilot in combat, speed is life.'

When engaging an enemy formation a pair of F-15s would make a high-speed charging attack, knocking down perhaps half a dozen aircraft with missiles and continuing on at high speed until out of reach of any counter-attack. Then, if the enemy formation maintained cohesion and was continuing towards its target, the process would be repeated.

The primary role of the F-15 is to destroy enemy bomb-carrying aircraft, avoiding escorting fighters if at all possible. But it is impossible to establish which blips on radar are from bombers and which from fighters, and there would be occasions when defending fighters became embroiled with enemy fighters bent on their destruction. If that happened, Chuck Casey would avoid a manoeuvring fight if he could, even though the F-15 can out-turn most types of aircraft it is likely to meet in combat. In a turning fight the F-15s could be vulnerable if other enemy fighters joined in the combat:

'Turning in one area like they did in the Battle of Britain, we call that 'anchoring the fight', we wouldn't want to do that. The F-15 would probably be the largest combat aircraft flying over Central Europe, it would be very visible. We might draw enemy fighters on to us. If we were ordered to defend an airfield or a specific area then, yes, we would turn in order to defend that point and shoot down as many enemy aircraft as we could. But the more turning we did, the more vulnerable our aircraft would become because they really are so very easy to see.

There could be occasions when we get involved in a turning fight whether we want to or not; if two aircraft pass each other head-on and one turns after the other's tail, the other pilot had better turn as well or he could be shot down. How long a turning fight would keep going would depend on the pilots involved, but I think neither side's fighter pilots would want to be in that sort of fight for long.

Our main tactic is the hit-and-run attack rather than the manoeuvring fight. However, the F-15 is extremely man-oeuvrable and a good dogfighter, and if we were forced into a turning fight we should be able to give the enemy fighters a hard time until we could break out.'

The escort of package formations deep into enemy territory is another role that F-15s would perform in war. As in the case of the German fighter pilots flying escort missions during the Battle of Britain in 1940, the USAF fighter pilots would not want to be tied too closely to their charges:

'Some strike leaders might like to have us attached to their formation, but I think that having sky-coloured F-15s going in at low altitude with the package might highlight its position. I would rather not be attached closely to the package because that would reduce my fighting capability to some extent. Given the choice I would rather go in a few minutes ahead of the package in a pre-strike sweep, or operate autonomously near the package with full freedom of action.'

The history of air combat provides numerous examples of occasions when well-trained pilots outfought a numerically superior enemy. To provide realistic training for its fighter pilots the USAF runs the so-called Aggressor programme, in which special units flying F-5s play the part of enemy fighters and use tactics similar to those employed by the Soviet Air Force. An ex-Aggressor pilot himself, Chuck Casey is a firm supporter of this type of training:

'If you are going to train the way you fight, it is important to simulate air combat as realistically as possible. The F-5, which we use to represent the MiG-21, is small and highly manoeuvrable like the Soviet fighter. It is a fairly good simulator of the MiG-21 even though it doesn't look like one.'

The Aggressor units provide a series of graded exercises ranging from the relatively simple to the extremely difficult, starting with a one versus one manoeuvring fight and working up to several aircraft versus several:

'There is very little training value to be gained from practising hit-and-run attacks, getting an opposing aircraft within range of our missiles, simulating launching and then leaving the area. We design our training combat scenarios to make people turn, but that is strictly to train pilots to fly the airplane effectively and get them out of situations which they might be forced into during a turning fight. Pilots are taught to manoeuvre in relation to another aircraft, to understand the capabilities of their own aircraft and to recognize what the other guy is doing.

The Aggressor programme has been very successful. When we entered the conflict in Vietnam most of our pilots did not have combat experience. The manoeuvring environment they found themselves in when they engaged the MiG-17, the MiG-19 and the MiG-21 was something they had not had a chance to practise. Nor was it our philosophy at the time to teach people to do that. Most of the guys had never simulated any kind of manoeuvring combat against aircraft types other than the one they were flying. Today I think our fighter pilots are far better prepared for air-to-air combat than they were before the conflicts in Korea and Vietnam. In peacetime they have had the chance to fly training exercises against an aircraft similar to those they might meet in combat. The confidence that gives is invaluable.'

4: The Long Punch

Lieutenant-Colonel Peter Granger joined the US Air Force in 1967. After completing pilot training he was sent to Vietnam where he flew Bird Dog spotter aircraft as a forward air controller, directing air strikes on targets close to friendly troops. In 1969 he returned to the USA and in 1972 went to the F-111 training school at Nellis, Nevada, where he underwent an operational conversion on this type. Early in 1973 he returned to South East Asia and flew the F-111 in action with the 442nd Tactical Fighter Squadron based at Takhli in Thailand. Later in the year he returned to Nellis to join the 442nd Tactical Fighter Training Squadron with F-111s. In 1977 he was posted to the 388th Tactical Fighter Squadron flying F-111s at Mountain Home, Idaho, and remained with the unit until 1979 when he went to staff college. On completion of the course he was posted to Headquarters Tactical Air Command at Langley, Virginia, where he served in the Directorate of Operations. In March 1983 he was posted to Upper Heyford in England, first as operations officer then as commander of the 79th Tactical Fighter Squadron equipped with F-111Es. At the time of writing he has nearly 2,000 hours' flying time in different versions of this aircraft.

The 79th is one of three tactical fighter squadrons, each established at twenty-four General Dynamics F-111Es, operating from Upper Heyford as part of the 20th Tactical Fighter Wing. The F-111E is a twin-engined, swing-wing heavyweight night and all-weather tactical attack bomber, capable of supersonic speed at all altitudes except at low level when carrying external bombs. It carries a crew of two, a pilot and a weapon systems officer (WSO) seated side by side, and in its combat configuration the aircraft has a take-off weight of nearly 40 tons.

The F-111 is by far the heaviest combat aircraft currently based in Western Europe, and it has a range and payload performance unequalled by any other combat aircraft in the theatre. Able to take off with up to 32,000 lb of fuel in its internal tanks and up to 8,000 lb of bombs on the underwing pylons, it is able to hit targets deep in Eastern Europe from bases in England without carrying external fuel tanks or resorting to in-flight refuelling. For such missions the F-111s would cross friendly territory at high altitude where their engines give the best fuel consumption, descending to low altitude before penetrating into enemy territory. After leaving enemy territory the aircraft would climb back to high altitude for the return flight. For operations against targets at even greater distances from base, these aircraft could carry external tanks or be refuelled in the air.

The F-111 dates back to the mid-1960s and the 'E' model carries essentially the same avionic equipment as was fitted to the original 'A' model. Thus although the aircraft's navigation and weapons-aiming systems were extremely advanced when the aircraft first entered service, they have since been overtaken by newer developments. This places the Upper Heyford crews at a very considerable disadvantage compared with those crews flying aircraft with more modern systems, as Peter Granger explained:

'The avionics systems fitted to the F-111E represent early-1960s technology, and the aircraft carries old analogue computers. The F-111Fs at Lakenheath have inertial navigation systems that use digital computers and are much more modern. So comparing our aircraft with those is like comparing an old Model A Ford with a modern Cadillac. The F-111F guys talk about working occasionally with degraded systems; we start out with degraded systems!'

The squadron commander listed the types of conventional weapon his aircraft would carry in action and which his crews are trained to use:

'Our F-111Es can carry 2,000 lb or 500 lb general purpose 'dumb' bombs, retarded or 'slick', or CBUs – cluster bomb units. For attacks on runways we also have the French Durandel cratering weapon. We do not have any guided weapons assigned to our squadron nor are my crews currently trained to use them.'

Typical attack loads for the F-111E making a high-speed, low-altitude penetration are four 2,000 lb bombs, or twelve 500 lb bombs, or twelve Durandels, or sixteen 750 lb cluster bomb units. Conventional (i.e. non-nuclear) bombs are carried externally on the four underwing pylons. The F-111 is fitted with a small internal bomb bay, but it is not normally used for conventional weapons because there is considerable turbulence if the bomb doors are opened when the aircraft is flying at high speed and low altitude.

Most of the types of conventional bombs carried by the 79th TFS are simple free-fall weapons, the only exception being the Durandel, a bomb of French design, built specifically to crater runways. These bombs weigh 440 lb each, and for a normal runway attack operation the F-111E would carry twelve on its underwing bomb pylons:

'Durandel has given a quantum jump to our ability to destroy runways. These bombs would be released in a line from low altitude, crossing the runway to be attacked at an oblique angle. As each one falls clear of the aircraft, a drogue parachute opens to retard the bomb and tip its nose towards the ground. When the bomb is pointing towards the ground the parachute is released and a rocket fires to drive the warhead clean through the concrete of the runway. After a short delay to give it time to get underneath the concrete, the warhead explodes. This will cause a massive upheaval of the runway and spread debris across the surface to prevent aircraft taking off or landing.'

The reader might be surprised to learn how limited and unsophisticated are the range of weapons carried by the F-111s of the 20th Tactical Fighter Wing. But it should be remembered that within NATO these aircraft are, in fact, part of an integrated force, in which it is not necessary for every type of aircraft to be able to undertake every role it is theoretically capable of doing:

'I think one of the hardest things about communicating the capabilities of the F-111E is that people tend to look at the brochure written by General Dynamics [the makers], and think the plane can do all the things it says in the book. But it seems that no government buys all the extras that can go with an airplane, any more than a car purchaser buys every item in the brochure list of extras.'

Peter Granger has no doubt that his aircraft would be extremely effective against the types of target best suited to them. He feels strongly that not only are there very definite limits on the effectiveness of air-to-ground missiles, but that there are certain types of target that are best dealt with using 'dumb bombs':

'To drop precision-guided munitions an aircraft has to climb to acquire its target. This means it has to expose itself above the terrain, and that could be very dangerous in some places. And for the optically guided missiles, clear skies are necessary in the target area. Guided weapons can be very accurate, but most of them are really expensive. If I can catch a concentration of vehicles, for example a convoy or a truck park or something like that, I will probably be able to attack it more effectively with a stick of cluster bombs than someone else could using far more expensive guided missiles.

The units employing precision-guided missiles are better than we are at hitting small, hard, pinpoint targets such as bridges. We should not be sent against a small bridge; that is not the best use of our capability. But if the nature and strength of the defences prevent a high angle of delivery, then all that is left is the low-altitude lay-down delivery mode which we do best. If you stay low, that increases your survivability.'

The sort of targets against which the F-111Es would be most effective include airfields, railway marshalling yards and junctions, and troop parks,.all of them relatively large static targets whose destruction would require large weights of conventional bombs. Single F-111s would also be effective against small, relatively soft pinpoint targets such as radar sites or radio communications stations:

'An airfield is an ideal sort of target for the F-111. We would not be able to take it out altogether, that would be a big job. But we could deny an enemy the use of an airfield for a period of time, say twelve hours. Some of our aircraft would drop Durandels to break up the runways; others would drop cluster bombs, the bomblets fused to go off if they were disturbed – if, for example, there was an attempt to repair the runway.

Our best capability is at night and in dirty weather, because under those conditions the defences are least effective against us. Under those conditions single aircraft would fly independently towards the same target, approaching it from different headings to make a co-ordinated attack. Operating in that way my squadron could put twelve airplanes across a target within three to four minutes.

However, we are not restricted to night operations. A lot would depend on whom we are supporting and what their needs are. Attacking targets by day, our aircraft would go in as two-ships, with minimum separation between attacks. I could see my aircraft being used in force package operations by day. We think in terms of a package that would include escorting fighters and 'Wild Weasel' people to suppress some of the defensive sites so that we can get to the target. And there are the EF-111s. We would like to think they might give us a clear avenue of approach through part of the defences. The number of F-111s sent against a target would depend on its size, and the weight of bombs necessary to inflict the required amount of damage.'

Peter Granger went on to outline the ways in which F-111 crews sought to avoid attack from enemy fighters and surface-to-air weapons:

'One of our most important self-protection features is the ability to fly very low and fast, at night and in poor weather. That is a tremendous self-protection feature. The F-111 will fly on automatic pilot controlled by the terrain-following radar at 200 to 300 feet at night. If anything goes wrong at low altitude at night, there is obviously very little time for the pilot to react before the aircraft hits the ground. But in war it is a lot more dangerous to fly slower or higher, so in the final analysis we would be much safer relying on our automatic systems.'

If its route has been planned carefully, the F-111E will approach its target low and fast under cover of darkness, making the most of the terrain. Under such conditions it can be engaged only on fleeting occasions, and then only by radar-controlled fighters or radar-directed surface anti-aircraft systems. To reduce the effectiveness of these the F-111E carries a range of electronic countermeasures systems: an ALQ-94 radar deception system built into the fuselage, an ALQ-119 jamming pod under the rear fuselage, and a radar warning receiver. The aircraft also carries chaff and infra-red decoy flares.

The F-111 is theoretically capable of exceeding the speed of sound at low altitude even carrying external bombs, but to reach such a speed the engines would devour prodigious amounts of fuel. This and other problems make it most unlikely that attack aircraft would reach such speeds during the penetration or attack phases of their missions:

'The F-111 is a good, fast airplane, but we would be hard pressed to go supersonic at low altitude carrying bombs on the external pylons. Even where the plane itself can go faster, we have to observe bomb carriage limiting speeds and, in the target area, bomb release limiting speeds. At very high speeds the airflow over the bombs can cause them to heat up, and that might mean that their fuses failed to function properly when they hit the target. Also, at very high speed you can get turbulent airflow across the bomb pylons and if the bombs are released then they may tumble as they fall away. That will decrease the accuracy of the bombs and perhaps cause them to miss the target altogether. In the case of retarded bombs released at too high a speed, the retarding fins might tear away and allow the bomb to go ballistic. The bomb could end up directly underneath the aircraft when it went off – you could take yourself out of the war doing that! So those weapon carriage and release speed limitations are things we have to respect.

High speed costs fuel, so we would go in at low altitude at 480 to 510 knots, in that region. If we go faster than that it costs a lot more fuel. Coming back with no bombs we could go supersonic at low altitude if we needed to avoid a threat, if our fuel reserves permitted.'

If it is pursued by enemy fighters, the F-111 flying close to the ground at high speed will provide a difficult target:

'Carrying a load with the wings swept aft to 45 degrees, the F-111 is a big, heavy, stable airplane. It's a smooth ride at high speed and low altitude, down where we can outrun just about any fighter. There are a few that can go as fast as we can low down, but they will have stability problems if they try to go after us. Most fighters have relatively low wing loadings, which means that their pilots would have a rough ride. Provided we do not turn we present a very small silhouette from the rear, which would make it very hard for enemy pilots to see us against the terrain.

I see most of us fighting at altitudes below 1,000 feet, going supersonic only as a dash on the return flight to escape from enemy fighters. If we were being engaged by surface-to-air missiles we would turn to put them on our beam, to make them overshoot – provided we detected them in time.'

Previous conflicts have shown clearly that a combination of high-speed, low-altitude flight using cover from the terrain, plus electronic jamming, chaff or infra-red decoy flares and a correctly executed evasive manoeuvre, will greatly reduce the chances of air-launched or surface-launched anti-aircraft missiles finding their target.

The aircraft of the 20th TFW lack the more exotic forms of weaponry carried by some of the other aircraft in the 2 ATAF order of battle. The navigation and bombing systems fitted to the F-111E are not the most modern, but they are adequate for attacks on any but the smallest and the hardest of targets. When handled by experienced crews and sent against suitable targets, there can be no doubt that these aircraft would prove extremely effective. They are able to penetrate enemy defences at low altitude, at night or in poor weather, flying at speeds often limited only by the carriage and release limits of the bombs themselves. The F-111 is able to carry useful loads of conventional bombs to targets anywhere in a European theatre of operations, supported where necessary by tanker aircraft.

In April 1986 the F-111 gave an impressive demonstration of its reach with in-flight refuelling, when aircraft of this type from Upper Heyford and Lakenheath attacked targets in Libya. The aircraft took a circuitous route around the west of Spain to avoid flying over mainland Europe, involving a round trip of more than 4,800 miles.

5: The Bridge Droppers

Lieutenant-Colonel Paul 'Zack' Fazackerley joined the US Air Force in 1967, and after completing his pilot training served in Vietnam flying as a forward air controller and in AC-130 gunships and KC-135 tanker aircraft. In 1972 he returned to the USA to take up a staff appointment at Strategic Air Command Headquarters, after which he flew FB-111 strategic bombers with 380th Bomb Wing at Plattsburg, New York. In 1978 he was appointed to the personnel office at the Pentagon, and remained there until 1982 when he went to the Armed Forces Staff College. Following that he was posted to Lakenheath in England, initially as assistant operations officer with the 494th Tactical Fighter Squadron equipped with F-111Fs. In May 1985 he was appointed commander of that unit.

The 494th Tactical Fighter Squadron is one of three F-111F squadrons, each established at twenty-four aircraft, which make up the 48th Tactical Fighter Wing based at Lakenheath in Suffolk. Externally the F-111F is similar to the E Model described in the previous chapter and has a similar performance, but it is fitted with a far more advanced electronic navigation and attack system and a Pave Tack pod for use with laser-guided bombs. These differences confer on the F-111F an ability to deliver precision attacks on targets deep in enemy territory which is unrivalled by any other aircraft type based in Western Europe.

The Pave Tack laser designating system weighs 1,300 lb and is housed in a streamlined pod just over 13 feet long, fitted under the centre fuselage of the F-111. At the rear end of the pod is the detecting set, the infra-red equivalent of a television camera with a zoom lens. The detecting set is mounted on gimbals to give freedom of movement and can be pointed in the required direction by the weapon systems officer in the aircraft by means of a small hand controller. The infra-red picture from the Pave Tack can be switched on to one of the TV-type screens in front of the weapon systems officer. In the middle of the screen is the aiming reticle, which indicates the point on the ground where the laser target designator is focused. By moving the apparent position of the target under the sighting reticle on his screen, the WSO can align the pod's laser designator on the target. If the laser is then switched on, a pencil-thin line of laser energy is beamed at the target. Laser-guided bombs released by the aircraft will home on the laser energy reflected off the target, and will impact within an extremely small circle of error – of the order of a few feet if the system is functioning properly and has been operated correctly. A video recorder built into the pod stores on film everything shown on the WSO's screen during the flight, for play-back and analysis after the aircraft has landed. Because it operates in the infra-red part of the frequency spectrum, Pave Tack is effective by night as well as by day. Infra-red energy cannot penetrate cloud or thick haze, however, and where these are present the system might not be usable.

For use with Pave Tack the F-111F can carry Paveway laser-guided bombs of various sizes. These bombs are not powered and to reach their target they depend on the forward speed imparted to them by the aircraft at the time of release. A typical war load for the F-111F is four 2,000 lb Paveway bombs carried on the underwing pylons. As operated by the 494th, the F-111F is also able to go into action carrying the same range of weapons as the 'E' model: the Durandel runway cratering bomb, various types of cluster bomb and non-guided general purpose 2,000 and 500 lb bombs.

'Our main mission is with Pave Tack, attacking precision targets with our laser-guided bombs. But if the bad guys start rolling through the Fulda Gap [in West Germany] and the weather at the targets is nasty, we're not going to sit on the ground waiting for the visibility to improve to the point where we can use Pave Tack. We're going to go ahead and fly missions with our other types of bomb.'

Because the combination of Pave Tack and laser-guidance can deliver bombs with such accuracy, it is tailor-made for attacks on such difficult targets as bridges, command post bunkers and specific targets on airfields such as underground fuel tanks, bomb and missile storage areas, hardened briefing facilities, etc. But almost certainly bridges would be the main targets for the F-111Fs during the early stages of any conflict in Europe. To bring down a strongly built bridge of steel, masonry or concrete it is necessary to hit it in exactly the right place with a large weight of explosive. Of the weapons currently in the 2 ATAF inventory, the laser-guided 2,000-pounder is by far the most effective against such a target. And the F-111F is the only aircraft in the force which can deliver this weapon against distant targets by night.

'Using Pave Tack we can put down bombs extremely accurately. If the target is a bridge, one is asking which part of the bridge is to be hit. It has to be carefully thought out. With the precision we have we can hit one end of a bridge, or any one span or supporting pillar. If we take out the centre span of a bridge, enemy engineers might be able to lay girders and metal plates over the hole so that vehicles could resume using it. If on the other hand we took one end off the bridge, that might give them a much more difficult repair problem. It all depends on the construction of the bridge we are attacking.'

If a target is undefended it would be a relatively simple matter for an F-111F to fly straight over it at medium altitude, mark the aiming point with the laser, release the bombs and hold the laser on the target until the bombs impacted. But all important targets in Eastern Europe would be surrounded by powerful anti-aircraft gun and missile defences, and any attack method which did not take this into account would be doomed to failure. Zack Fazackerley outlined the type of attack his unit would employ when going against a defended target with laser-guided bombs; the low-flying tactics to penetrate the outer defences and approach the target would be similar to those used by other types of attack aircraft:

'When we fly at night and in poor weather, we use terrain-following radar in automatic flight at low altitude. Usually we fly as single ships. We can go together in pairs for mutual support, but still the aircraft would navigate and attack independently.

Our plan is to go in underneath the enemy radars, unseen, at very high speed. Even if we were seen by enemy radars, we would be going so fast and using the terrain to mask us so that they would soon lose us. That is our best offensive tactic. If I am put in against a target at night and in poor weather I don't fear any defensive system, missiles or fighters.'

For self-protection the F-111F carries the same electronic coun-termeasures equipment as the E model, supplemented by a couple of AIM-9L Sidewinder missiles for self-defence against enemy fighters.

Having penetrated the defences the F-111F would make for an initial point (IP) near the target, a distinctive navigation feature which the weapon systems officer could use to up-date his navigation. From the IP, the attack is rather different from those by aircraft carrying other types of weapon:

'We would aim to get to our IP accurately, using radar and turn in for our attack run flying at between 200 and 400 feet using the terrain-following radar and accelerating to about 600 knots. At a pre-computed distance from the target, I would pull the aircraft into a 4-g climb and by then my WSO should see the target on his radar. The bombs are released shortly after beginning the pull-up – the lower we are when we release them, the less we expose ourselves to the defences. Once the bombs are off we want to get back to low altitude as soon as we can. I will roll the aircraft into a wing-over and pull it into a turn.

Up to the time of bomb release the WSO does not usually see the target on Pave Tack, but aims the bombs using radar. The object is to give the bombs enough velocity to take them past the target, and use the laser guidance to pull them down on the target. (The bombs are not powered; if they begin to fall short of the target we can't give them extra speed.) We would release the laser-guided bombs with an interval of a few milliseconds between each, to separate them and prevent them colliding in flight.'

The attack phase of the Pave Tack mission imposes a tremendous workload on the two-man crew of the F-111F. They have to work together closely to perform a complex series of operations accurately and in the right order. Flying on instruments without reference to external features, the pilot has to take the aircraft through a carefully programmed three-dimensional manoeuvre involving simultaneous changes of direction, altitude and attitude. All this has to be done while flying dangerously

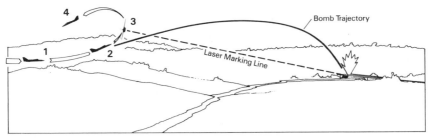

F–111F attack with laser-guided bomb
1. Aircraft approaches target at low altitude.
2. At a previously computed distance from target, the aircraft pulls up into 4 g climb and lobs its bombs in the direction of the target several miles away.
3. After releasing its bombs, the aircraft banks steeply, turns through 90 degrees and flies tangentally to the target, to allow the weapon systems officer to hold the laser designator on the target throughout the flight of the bombs.
4. When the bombs impact the aircraft returns to low altitude and makes its getaway

close to the ground, and in wartime he might have somebody shooting at him. Meanwhile the weapon systems officer, having switched the Pave Tack picture on to the TV screen in front of him, moves his stick controller to bring the target's apparent position under the sighting reticle in the centre of the screen. Once the reticle is over the target he switches on the laser to mark the aiming point for the salvo of bombs already in flight, and holds the reticle on the target until the bombs impact. The two crewmen have quite different tasks to perform, but they have to co-ordinate their actions if the attack is to be successful:

'The pilot has to consider the terrain around him, because he could be flying the manoeuvre at night. Once he starts the pull-up he is off terrain-following radar, so he needs to know when he can start his recovery turn and not fly into a hill. He needs to know when to stop the climb and begin pulling into a wing-over and then start the turn to bring the aircraft around to the egress heading. The manoeuvre is not that difficult, it is a fairly standard manoeuvre. But it has to be done right, and at night or in poor weather it is definitely not what you would consider a natural act.

Meanwhile the guy in the right seat, the WSO, while being pulled and twisted and turned upside down, is looking at the target on the Pave Tack picture on his main screen. The Pave Tack has a narrow field of view and he has to align the sighting reticle on the target very precisely. It is almost like looking down through a soda straw.'

The extremely accurate attacks which are possible using Pave Tack with laser-guided bombs would make the F-111F devastatingly effective in time of war. Few pinpoint targets, however well hardened, can survive one or more 2,000 lb bombs impacting on their weakest point:

'Delivering laser-guided bombs at night is an extremely demanding exercise which requires precise execution and a high degree of crew co-ordination. We have to couple the use of the radar and the Pave Tack, get everything done precisely and in sequence, and spot the target and track it. The final pay-off is that you save effort, because a target can be destroyed in one sortie instead of many. But the price you have to pay is the training to develop the capability to do that. An enormous amount of very specialized training is necessary before a crew can perform the Pave Tack mission.'

Pave Tack is a versatile piece of equipment. As well as assisting bombing it confers on the F-111F a useful day-and-night reconnaissance capability, and it can be used to assist with navigation at night:

> 'The most important use of Pave Tack is to provide laser guidance for bombs to destroy our targets. But we video record everything we do, so it is very handy for bomb damage assessment. The picture shows how well the WSO was able to track the target and where the bombs impacted. Afterwards we can play back the film and assess the amount of damage inflicted. If we were asked to, while over enemy territory on our way back from targets we could use Pave Tack to look at bridges and airfields hit during other attacks, to see the extent of the damage or the progress of repairs.'

F-111Fs from Lakenheath took part in the attack on Tripoli in April 1986 and scored hits with Paveway laser-guided bombs on Colonel Gadafy's headquarters and other targets. Afterwards Pave Tack film of the attacks was shown during television news broadcasts.

A high level of skill is necessary for a crew to be able to laser mark a defended target and carry out an accurate attack using laser-guided bombs. Because of this, a long period of highly specialized training is necessary before an F-111F crew becomes proficient in the role:

> 'Not everyone in my squadron is capable of flying Pave Tack missions, but our objective is to train people to do that. Ours is the only base in the world with F-111F, the F model is the only F-111 with Pave Tack. So new pilots or WSOs joining the wing at Lakenheath have to learn to operate a different type of F-111, then they have to learn to use Pave Tack. We get a lot of inexperienced WSOs; they have to learn to read the radar picture and identify land targets with precision, and transition from that to the Pave Tack picture. It takes about a year from the time a guy comes to Lakenheath until he is qualified to fly all of our roles including the Pave Tack mission. On my squadron I have twenty-five WSOs. Usually I can get about

fifteen of those qualified to operate the entire weapons system.'

Those crews not qualified to carry out missions using Pave Tack
would be assigned to attacks using bombs without laser guidance.

Zack Fazackerley has great confidence in the ability of the
F-111 to carry out its role of long-range attack at night or in poor
weather, against pinpoint targets. Even though it has been in
service a long time, he does not think it is overshadowed by any
of the newer types:

'The F-111 is no longer a new aircraft, but the F model has
greatly improved avionics compared with the earlier versions
and it will continue in service for a long time yet. It is the only
aircraft assigned to NATO which can attack targets in
Eastern Europe from bases in England, flying at very low level
at night and in poor weather. And of course we carry Pave
Tack, which greatly enhances our capability.'

Like other officers interviewed, Zack Fazackerley did not
consider a major war in Europe to be likely unless there was
some gross miscalculation by one side or the other:

'I was on holiday in Leningrad in 1984, at the time of the 40th
anniversary of the lifting of the siege. We in the West tend to
see the Russian bear as a big bad bear, an aggressive animal.
After being there and listening to the Russians, looking at
their technology and the way they live, seeing how they view
NATO and the West, and China, I think they maintain a
strong capability because they are determined never again to
let themselves be rolled over as they were by the Germans in
the Second World War. It is only a personal opinion, but I
don't think the Russians are at all likely to move against the
West. I think they would have to feel very threatened indeed
before they made any attempt to take on NATO.'

6: The Airfield Bashers

Wing Commander Grant McLeod joined the Royal Air Force as a Cranwell cadet in 1964. On completion of pilot training he flew Canberras on second-line tasks with No. 98 Squadron, then with No. 360 Squadron in the electronic warfare training role. In 1969 he re-trained for the ground attack role and flew Hunters with Nos 45 and 58 Squadrons. In 1974 he converted to the Phantom and joined No. 17 Squadron in Germany flying this aircraft in the ground attack role. Early in 1976 he converted to the Jaguar and returned to Germany to fly in the same roles with No. 31 Squadron. In 1978 he was promoted to Squadron Leader and took command of No. 63 Squadron at the Tactical Weapons Unit instructing ground attack pilots. There followed a staff tour, then he attended the British Army Staff College. In 1984 he was promoted to Wing Commander, converted to the Tornado, and took command of No. 17 Squadron forming with the new type at Brüggen in Germany.

No. 17 Squadron is based at Brüggen in western Germany, close to the border with Holland, and is equipped with the Panavia Tornado GR1 which it operates in the attack role. The Tornado GR1 is a twin-engined swing-wing, medium-weight night and all-weather tactical attack bomber, built under a tri-national programme by Great Britain, Germany and Italy. The aircraft carries a crew of two, a pilot and a navigator, and is equipped for high-speed, low-altitude precision-attack operations. In its combat configuration the aircraft takes off at a weight of about 27 tons.

Having amassed more than 2,800 hours flying four generations of ground attack aircraft in the Royal Air Force, Grant McLeod has seen at first hand the progressive improvements in navigation systems and the effect this has had on operational capability:

'The Hunter was a very simple aircraft and navigation was by map and stop watch. Even in good weather it was hard work for the pilot to get himself to the target area, find the pull-up point, get his sight on the target and attack with guns or rockets or bombs, then navigate home. Whether a pilot was successful in doing this depended to a great extent on his level of skill and experience.

The Phantom was a lot better. It carried a navigator, and there was a first-generation analogue computer and an early inertial navigation system to help us get to our targets and we could do so considerably more accurately and in rather worse weather than was possible in the Hunter.

The Jaguar was only a single-seater, but it was a better attack aircraft than the Phantom. It had a much more accurate inertial navigation system and a digital computer which could hold a lot more data and digest new data much more quickly. What that meant, in simple terms, was that in a Jaguar the average pilot was able to find his target in worse weather, and drop his bombs with greater accuracy, than he could have in a Hunter or a Phantom.

The Tornado navigation system is a similar order of advance over that in the Jaguar. In terms of capability and accuracy, comparing the Tornado navigation system with the one I flew with in the Phantom is like comparing an old-fashioned pocket watch with a modern multi-function digital. It enables the Tornado to hit targets accurately in the worst of weather or at night.

What difference does it make to the crew to have the more modern system? It is a question of workload. The Tornado crew can hand over much of the routine navigation of the aircraft to the computer. They can let the computer navigate them to the target, confident that they are flying clear of known defended areas, on track and on time. That is a tremendous advantage. It gives the crew more time to manage their weapons system, the navigator can spend more time looking at his radar to up-date his computer, managing his electronic countermeasures equipment, keeping watch for enemy fighters, etc. It has taken a lot of the cockpit workload out of basic navigation. The bottom line of this is that we now

see relatively inexperienced crews flying Tornado and producing quite outstanding bombing results.'

The Tornado's ability to attack targets with great accuracy
has given a new lease of life to the old-fashioned general-purpose
bomb. When carrying this type of weapon a normal attack
configuration for the aircraft is four 1,000-pounders under the
fuselage and a drop tank, a Sidewinder missile and an electronic
countermeasures pod under each wing. If used properly a
1,000 lb bomb has sufficient destructive power to wreck most
types of target, but only if it scores a direct hit or a fairly near
miss. An often-quoted adage on bombing accuracy states that if
the average bomb-aiming error throughout a raiding force can
be halved, the effect of a given weight of attack will be
quadrupled; so money spent on reducing bombing errors is
usually money well spent:

'Yes, the Tornado is a very expensive aeroplane. But against
a given target one needs fewer Tornadoes to achieve a given
amount of damage than if older types such as Phantoms or
Jaguars were used: the Tornado weapon aiming system is so
much more accurate that a far lower proportion of the bombs
will miss the target and be wasted.'

A further advantage conferred by the Tornado's advanced
navigational system is that it enables the aircraft to attack at
night or in far worse weather than its predecessors could. Under
such conditions it is much more difficult for enemy anti-aircraft
defences to interfere with an attack and prevent accurate
bombing.
   Typical of the high-value targets the Royal Air Force Tornadoes might be sent against are airfields, a task for which they are
uniquely well equipped. Even with the most modern weaponry
these are difficult targets, however:

'Look at a plan of a typical modern hardened military airfield
and you will see it has certain characteristics. The runway is
longer and much wider than necessary for take-offs and
landings, so that even if part of it is cratered a usable strip

might remain. Parallel to the runway is a taxiway long enough for aircraft to take off and land. There are individual concrete shelters for the aircraft, dispersed over a large area. Thick layers of concrete protect the operations room and other vital points. The bulk fuel installation is buried and hardened, and split into well-separated parts so that if part of the installation is damaged the aircraft can continue operating. Bomb and missile storage areas are similarly protected. Refuelling vehicles, weapon loading equipment and other items important for the operation of aircraft are dispersed over a wide area.'

Modern air attack planning is an exact science which must take into account the limitations of the various weapon systems. To take a major enemy airfield as an example, although militarily it might be highly desirable to render it unusable for a long period, say a couple of weeks, that would require a force far larger than is ever likely to be available:

'A plan to close an airfield for many days might require the use of a hundred aeroplanes, and almost certainly there would not be a hundred aeroplanes that could be spared for that purpose. From that it follows that we cannot reasonably expect to be able to close an airfield for that period.'

Nor is it likely that enemy aircraft on the ground at such an airfield would present profitable targets:

'The days are long past when one could expect to find enemy aircraft parked on the ground in neat rows. Nowadays all major air forces disperse their aircraft around the airfield in individual hardened shelters which are strong enough to withstand anything but a direct hit or a very near miss from a large bomb. A raiding force running in to attack aircraft in their shelters would have no way of knowing which shelters contained aircraft and which were empty. So to destroy a large proportion of the aircraft on the airfield the attacking force would have to destroy a large proportion of the shelters. Again, that would probably require an attack force too large to be worthwhile.'

Having mentioned a couple of areas to avoid when planning an attack on an airfield, Grant McLeod went on to outline those parts of the target system against which telling blows could be struck. With its very accurate aiming system the Tornado could mount toss-bombing attacks on important installations on the airfield, such as the fuel and munitions storage areas and headquarters bunkers.

For attacks on runways the Royal Air Force Tornado squadrons have recently received a specialized and extremely potent new weapon, the JP233. Each JP233 container is shaped like a flattened cigar about 2 feet high and 21 feet long, and holds 30 cratering bombs and 215 small mines; the Tornado carries two such containers side-by-side under the fuselage.

The JP233 runway-cratering bomb is about the size and shape of a road-mender's pneumatic drill without the bit and weighs about 57 lb. After it leaves its container a parachute opens to reduce its speed and point the nose towards the ground. When the bomb strikes a runway a small directional charge punches a narrow hole through the concrete, and injects a secondary warhead underneath the runway. After a short delay the secondary warhead detonates and the force of the explosion, contained between the underside of the runway and the foundations, produces an underground cavity topped with a hole and surrounded by an area of 'heave' – cracked and broken concrete pushed up from below. Aircraft attempting to move over 'heaved' areas could suffer severe damage to their undercarriages and might even break through into the foundations below. To restore such areas to use would require a lot of work: before the holes could be filled, the areas of cracked concrete would first have to be cut away and a large amount of debris removed.

If that was all there was to JP233, any organization charged with repairing its effects would face severe enough problems. But with the 60 cratering bombs from a pair of JP233 containers there would be 430 small mines, which would end up scattered amongst the rubble and craters to menace the repair teams. JP233 is a fiendish weapon, designed to put a runway out of action for as long as possible and to make repair as difficult and as dangerous as human ingenuity and low cunning can make it.

Typically an airfield-attack force might include eight Tornadoes carrying JP233, which would put down a total of 480 cratering bombs and 3,440 mines. Given sufficient resources, time and determination, engineers should be able to bring the runway and taxiways back into use after an attack of this type. But their work would probably not go unhindered:

'Such attacks would have to be repeated at intervals, and from then on the effect of the damage would be cumulative. If one of our raids caught their damage repair organization in the open, filling craters from a previous attack, we might be able to destroy their specialized plant – concrete mixers, bulldozers etc. If that happened we would know that the next time we raided them, they might not have enough plant to repair the damage in a short time and it would take the airfield much longer to recover from such an attack.

The idea is to damage the airfield, let the enemy begin to repair some of the facilities, then go back later and hit them again. They begin to repair that damage and we hit them yet again. If we could keep that up over a period the condition of the airfield would deteriorate rapidly. It would be rather like a boxer taking a pasting from his opponent: after he gets a bloody nose and a cut above his right eye, he becomes a lot less aggressive as the fight goes on.'

So long as the airfield lacked a length of concrete which its aircraft could reach, and which was long enough for them to take off, scores of enemy attack aircraft could be confined to the ground, perhaps during a crucial phase of the land battle.

As Air Marshal Hine outlined in Chapter 1, attack aircraft sent against heavily defended targets might be accompanied by escort fighters, jamming escorts and 'Wild Weasel' defence suppression aircraft to make the defenders' task more difficult. Operating with or without such support, Tornadoes would rely on accurate navigation to pick their way between heavily defended areas at low altitude, using high speed and their self-protection electronic countermeasures systems to penetrate those defended areas that they could not avoid:

'We would hope to get information from our various intelligence sources on where enemy anti-aircraft defences were concentrated. If we knew where they were, we could avoid those sources of danger. Precise navigation, coupled with the use of our radar warning receiver, would greatly reduce the risk to us. In the Tornado we can fly precise routes at night or in poor weather with a high degree of confidence.'

In time of war, attacks on NATO runways would have to be expected, possibly with specialized runway-cratering bombs and area-denial mines not unlike those put down by JP233. The Tornado was designed for the European theatre of operations and needs only a relatively short length of concrete to take off or land, the sort that might be left usable or which could be repaired rapidly after an attack on its base airfield. With its wings swung forward the Tornado has comparatively low take-off and landing speeds and, unique amongst NATO combat aircraft, its engines are fitted with thrust reversers to bring it to a halt after a short landing run.

Grant McLeod had no doubts on the best way to use the Tornado in war:

'If I had to go to war in a Tornado the time I would want to do it would be on a very dark night or in bad weather, along a route I had been able to study. If my navigator and I had had time to plan the attack in detail, with the high-quality radar and navigation systems of the Tornado, I am confident we would be able to find the target and hit it accurately. If we were used at times when it was impossible for enemy fighters to make visual attacks, or ground defences to engage with optically-laid weapons, I am confident that Tornadoes would get through to hit their targets. And when they did they would cause a hell of a lot of damage where it hurts most.'

7: The Carpet-Bombers

Oberstleutnant (Lieutenant-Colonel) Walter Jertz joined the Luftwaffe in 1965. After completing training as an F-104 pilot, in 1969 he joined Jagdbombergeschwader (Fighter Bomber Wing) 31 'Boelcke' operating in the nuclear strike and ground attack roles. From then until 1976 he held a succession of increasingly senior flying posts within the Geschwader, before he was promoted to Major and left the unit to spend two years at the German Armed Forces staff college. Following the course he returned to the Geschwader and commanded one of its two Staffeln. In 1981 he was promoted to Oberstleutnant and appointed to the staff of headquarters 3rd Air Division, where one of his responsibilities was to oversee the introduction of the Tornado into service in the Luftwaffe. In 1982 he returned to Jagdbombergeschwader 31 as deputy commander of operations, and in 1983 he became its Kommandeur Fliegende Gruppe (head of operations).

Jagdbombergeschwader 31 is based at Nörvenich near Cologne and has an established strength of thirty-eight Tornado attack aircraft. The Tornado operated by the German Air Force is almost identical to the attack version of this aircraft operated by the Royal Air Force and it is used for similar roles: offensive counter-air operations and interdiction missions against targets well behind the battle area, flown at night or in poor weather. Like his British counterpart, Walter Jertz is adamant that it would be a waste of resources to use an expensive aircraft like the Tornado for tasks that could be done as well or better by cheaper types of aircraft:

'We are trained to attack targets under the direction of a forward air controller, but unless there is a major crisis in the land battle I do not think we should be used for close air support. Simpler and cheaper types of aircraft like the A-10,

Alphajet or Harrier are perfectly suitable for daylight attacks on targets in and immediately behind the battle area. We would not like to fly against battlefield targets by day because we would be operating in an environment where everybody was shooting at us and we would get little or no advantage from our advanced electronic systems.'

As well as sophisticated ground-mapping radar and inertial navigation equipment, the Tornado has an integrated system linking the terrain-following radar, navigation computer and automatic pilot, which can fly the aircraft at high speed at 200 feet without the pilot touching the controls. Thus the aircraft can hug the ground shielded by darkness or poor visibility, safe from many forms of attack. When the Tornado is flying on automatic terrain-following the pilot can select one of three types of 'ride': soft, medium and hard. The soft ride is selected when the aircraft is passing over relatively lightly defended areas; the aircraft follows the general line of the contours and fairly gently smooths over hills and obstacles in its path without trying to follow their contours too abruptly. The hard ride setting is selected when the aircraft passes over heavily defended areas, when it is essential to follow undulations in the ground as closely as possible to exploit their cover to the full; but there is a limit to the amount of time the crew can stand being bounced about in this way. The medium ride setting is for use when conditions are between the two extremes. During the terrain-following phase of the flight, the computer also directs the autopilot to fly the aircraft along the track programmed by the aircraft's weapon systems officer.

In service the Tornado's automatic terrain-following system has proved extremely reliable. Nevertheless, pilots need a period of indoctrination before they are asked to entrust their lives to it:

'You have to learn to trust the system, you don't just get into the aircraft and fly on terrain-following radar at 200 feet at night. You start off by flying the aircraft on automatic terrain-following at 1,000 feet by day to give you confidence that the system really works. During our initial daylight flights we point the aircraft at high towers and hills to see if the terrain-following radar reacts, and of course it does. Then we take the aircraft down in steps to 500 feet, that is as low as we are allowed to fly with it over Germany in peacetime. When you have flown with it at low altitude often enough you come to trust the system. Then you do the same thing at night. Finally the crews go to Goose Bay [in Canada] where they can fly over uninhabited areas at 200 feet at night or in poor weather. Flying at low altitude in the Tornado is very smooth; if there is turbulence the automatic command stability and augmentation system will smooth out the bumps. As a pilot I don't like to have to admit it, but in this case the computer is better at flying the aircraft than I am.'

Before he converted to the Tornado, Walter Jertz flew the single-seat F-104 in the daylight nuclear strike and ground attack roles. Although the Tornado has very much more advanced navigation and weapon aiming systems than the F-104, he feels strongly that for night or poor weather operations a second crewman is essential if the new aircraft is to be flown to its full capability:

'In my opinion, having a second man in the aircraft gives a tremendous increase in capability. Being able to share the workload means the pilot can put emphasis on other things, like flying the aircraft very low and flying it safely. If you are flying at 200 feet at 540 knots you don't have much time to look into the cockpit. If I could talk to my computer and tell it to 'Select No. 2 bomb now' or 'Check my 6 o'clock [rear] for enemy fighters' and the computer could do it, then I might not need a WSO. If the aircraft had a computer that could talk to me like another man, it might be sufficient to have only one guy flying the aircraft. But computers can't do that. Maybe in ten or fifteen years computers will be able to, but they can't yet.'

At the time of writing, the German Air Force does not have a specialized runway attack weapon to compare with the JP233, though one is under development. Its Tornado units have recently started to receive the MW-1, a devastatingly effective area attack weapon for use against concentrations of enemy

˙vehicles and tanks. The MW-1 was tailored to fit below the flat underfuselage of the Tornado and comprises a streamlined container slightly longer than a Volvo estate wagon, with the width and depth of an average-sized kitchen table. A range of specialized sub-munitions has been developed for use with the MW-1 and containers with three types of load are currently in service in the German Air Force: with about 4,500 armour-piercing bomblets for use against tanks; with about 650 frag-mentation bomblets; and with a mixed load of about 2,250 anti-tank bomblets and 500 anti-tank mines (the exact figures are classified). The weight of an MW-1 container varies with the type of sub-munitions carried, but is about 4½ tons.

To put down such a large number of sub-munitions effectively over the target area the MW-1 employs a novel method of dispensing them. The sub-munitions are housed in packs, in 112 horizontal tubes each 132 mm (5.2 in.) in diameter running the width of the main container at right angles to the aircraft's line of flight. In the centre of each tube is an explosive charge, and the sub-munitions are loaded on either side of it. When the charge is fired the sub-munitions are forced violently outwards, away from each other and out at the sides of the container; each load cancels out the recoil force from the other, so there is no undue strain on the aircraft's structure. The largest charge used will fire the sub-munitions approximately 250 metres to each side of the aircraft, giving a maximum width to the pattern of bomblets of about 500 metres. There is a range of different explosive charges in the tubes and when they are fired at carefully controlled intervals the MW-1 distributes its sub-munitions in a fairly even pattern over a wide area.

The density of the carpet of bomblets put down by the MW-1 depends on the type of sub-munition used. In the case of the armour-piercing bomblets, for example, to knock out a tank one of these has to score a direct hit on the hull. When used against such targets the MW-1 can be programmed to fire all 4,500 anti-tank bomblets in just over half a second, to cover an area of approximately 500 metres by 180 metres – about twice the length and twice the width of a football field. This gives an average of one bomblet per 20 square metres – the approximate area of a medium tank – and would result in hits on a very high proportion of the vehicles within the area covered by the bomb carpet.

MW-1 fragmentation bomblets are effective against soft-skinned vehicles or troops if they come down within a few yards of them, so with this sub-munition a much lower density of bomblets is required and a container load can be spread over a far greater area. By increasing the total time over which the MW-1 is fired, the carpet of bomblets can be spread over a considerably greater distance. The length and density of the bomblet pattern is selected by the WSO prior to the attack, and controlled by the aircraft's weapon aiming computer. Only the selected number of sub-munitions will be fired during an attack; the others can be used for subsequent attacks.

The MW-1 puts out a wide spread of munitions on either side of the aircraft's flight path, a feature which allows Tornadoes to attack at right angles to a road being used by the enemy. This makes it difficult to position anti-aircraft defences to meet such a threat, because it is impossible to cover every part of a column of vehicles moving forward.

Apart from restricting the aircraft to a maximum speed of 600 knots, the huge MW-1 container causes remarkably little de-terioration in the Tornado's handling characteristics:

'Fully loaded the MW-1 container weighs about 4½ tons, but it does not make much difference to the handling of the aircraft because the Tornado's computer-controlled stability augmentation system is able to adjust for it. The normal tactics for use with the MW-1 are to fly over the target at more than 500 knots at 150 feet to lay down the pattern of sub-munitions. When the MW-1 container is empty it is jettisoned.

An ideal target for the MW-1 is a concentration of vehicles, attacked at night or in bad weather when they don't expect us. Because we can fight at night when their troops would be moving up, we could be very dangerous to the enemy.'

When sent to engage an enemy column at night with the MW-1, the Tornadoes would usually fly in units of two or four aircraft:

'When making for the target area at night or in poor weather we would observe the old German military adage, *getrennt marschieren, vereint schlagen* [split up for the march, concentrate for the attack]. So aircraft would fly singly, and come together at the target.

Using its computerized system the Tornado is able to navigate to designated points exactly, plus or minus zero seconds. Typically we would fly two aircraft and two a few miles behind, a maximum of four on the same route using what we call parallel tracking: pairs of aircraft flying one mile to either side of that common track to make sure they do not hit each other. In that way the aircraft can fly in formation without having to see each other or break radio silence.'

Carrying an attack load a Tornado normally flies with its wings swept back at 45 degrees, to give a good turning performance at low altitude. When passing through defended areas or if it is threatened by enemy fighters the aircraft will sweep its wings further back and accelerate:

'The normal cruising speed for the Tornado is 450 knots, increased to go through the FLOT [forward line of own troops]. Once past the FLOT we would throttle back to a speed which gives the best compromise between the requirements of survivability on the one hand, and fuel consumption and therefore combat range on the other. If I was intercepted by an enemy fighter I would accelerate to 600 knots and put my wings fully back to 67 degrees. A Tornado flying at 200 feet at that speed at night or in poor visibility is very difficult for a fighter to catch.'

Although the German Tornadoes would normally carry a pair of Sidewinder air-to-air missiles, whenever possible Walter Jertz would avoid contact with enemy aircraft.

'Our primary goal is to put the bombs on the target, and bring the aircraft back so it can be used for the next mission. It is not our task to look for a fight with enemy aircraft. We would engage them only if they attacked us, or if one appeared in front of us and we could shoot it down easily. That is why we train in defensive rather than offensive air fighting manoeuvres.'

To protect the aircraft against enemy radar-laid guns and homing missiles, German Tornadoes carry a Cerberus electronic countermeasures pod under one wing, and a chaff and infra-red decoy flare dispensing pod under the other.

To use the MW-1 to its full potential the Tornado crews would need up-to-the-minute information on the position of the enemy column, especially if it was on the move. This could come from the Tornado's own attack radar, which has sufficient discrimination for the WSO to see vehicles moving along a road. Or the Tornadoes could operate in conjunction with an RF-4C aircraft flying several minutes ahead of them, using its Pave Tack infra-red reconnaissance system to search likely routes for enemy troop movements. Such information would be broadcast in code to the aircraft in the attack force (for a description of this type of operation from the RF-4C viewpoint, see Chapter 10):

'If in the air we get last-minute information on the position of a suitable target, it is easy for a WSO to put the new target co-ordinates into his attack computer. We even have a mode of operation which allows us to be radar-silent during the last portion of our attack run, so we do not have to emit signals which might warn the enemy we were coming. We put the co-ordinates of the points of high ground into the navigation computer, and tell the computer to avoid those points. The computer will then direct the autopilot to steer the aircraft to avoid those points and we don't have to use the radar. We have done trials with the method and it works.'

Before a Tornado can make an attack using the MW-1 it has to release its underwing drop tanks, or they might be hit by some of the sub-munitions fired sideways. When the MW-1 container is empty it is jettisoned, to leave a clean aircraft that is perfectly capable of supersonic speed at low altitude if necessary. The shock wave thus produced could produce considerable damage on the ground:

'With the wings swept back at 67 degrees, an unloaded Tornado can exceed Mach 1 at low level. A few years ago the German Air Force did some trials using an F-104 flying supersonic at low level, to see what damage the shock wave would do. We found it will do quite a lot of damage; it can even turn over soft-skinned vehicles such as cars or trucks. Against troops in the open it will cause a period of disorientation and some may suffer ear damage. The shock wave does not cost very much because you are not using a bomb, and it does not need to be aimed with pinpoint accuracy. But to fly supersonic at low altitude the aircraft uses a lot of fuel so you cannot do it for long.'

As well as the MW-1 the German Air Force Tornado units are equipped with the usual range of general-purpose bombs: 1000-, 500-, and 250-pounders, both retarded and non-retarded, and BL755 cluster bombs. As Walter Jertz points out, if they can be put down on or sufficiently close to suitable targets the older types of bomb are still very effective:

'The accuracy of the Tornado weapon aiming system enables us to make effective use of the older types of bomb. We can make lay-down attacks with retarded bombs, or loft attacks using non-retarded weapons where the forward speed of the bomb might be needed to give it penetrating power. The accuracy of loft attacks is less than for a lay-down attack, but they have the advantage that you don't have to fly right over the target.'

Of the non-nuclear aircraft weapon systems available to NATO, the devastating combination of Tornado and MW-1 is by far the most efficient means of hitting enemy reinforcing units in rear areas moving forwards. This ability to put down a carpet of destruction on targets in defended areas has resurrected an air power option which had lain dormant since the demise of the Allied heavy bomber fleets after the end of the Second World War. And it has increased the ability of modern air power to exert decisive influence on the land battle without recourse to nuclear weapons. The German Tornadoes' main role would be to deliver their sledgehammer blows against troop and vehicle concentrations in the enemy rear areas, at night or in poor weather when there would be relatively little risk to the aircraft from the defences. At the beginning of this account Walter Jertz stressed that in his view the use of expensive Tornadoes in the close air support role, to attack individual tanks dispersed in the battle area by day, would be a misuse of resources. When one considers the alternative his unit can offer, it is difficult to disagree with him.

8: The Jump-Jet Dimension

Air Commodore Dick Johns joined the RAF in 1957 as a Cranwell cadet, and on completion of his pilot training flew Javelin night fighters with No. 64 Squadron. He then moved to the fighter-reconnaissance role and spent two years flying Hunters in Aden. Following his return to England he became a flying instructor, with one tour at Valley and a second at Cranwell. He then served on the Queen's Flight for a short time, before, in 1970, being appointed personal flying instructor to Prince Charles. In 1975 he took command of No. 3 Squadron flying Harriers in Germany. On his return to England in 1978 he moved into a staff appointment at the Ministry of Defence in London. In 1982, with the rank of Group Captain, he took command of the RAF Germany Harrier force and the important base at Gütersloh; in this chapter he describes some of the ways in which the Harrier's unique operating features might be used in time of war. Dick Johns returned to England in 1984 and is currently serving at the Royal College of Defence Studies in London.

The Royal Air Force Harrier Force in Germany comprises Nos 3 and 4 Squadrons, each established at eighteen Harriers. The British Aerospace Harrier is a single-seat, single-engined light attack bomber and reconnaissance aircraft, capable of vertical take-off and landing. In its usual combat configuration the aircraft weighs about 10 tons, but at that weight a short ground run is necessary before it can get airborne. The Harrier would usually operate only by day. In horizontal flight this aircraft is unable to exceed the speed of sound, but at low altitude carrying a war load the Harrier is as fast as any other modern attack aircraft similarly laden. Its normal armament is four or five BL755 cluster bombs, each containing 147 anti-tank bomblets, and two 30 mm cannon. All Harriers carry a built-in sideways-looking camera and thus have a photographic reconnaissance capability during normal attack missions; when operating solely in the reconnaissance role, however, the aircraft is fitted with an under-fuselage pod carrying five optical cameras to give horizon-to-horizon cover.

The main role of No. 3 Squadron is ground attack; the roles of No. 4 Squadron are ground attack and battlefield reconnaissance. During normal peacetime conditions the Harrier Force is based at Gütersloh near Bielefeld, some seventy nautical miles or an easy ten minutes' flying time from the East German border. When the Harrier Force deployed off base Dick Johns would go with it, after handing command of Gütersloh airfield to his deputy.

Before describing the new dimension the Harrier has brought to air operations, Dick Johns outlined the sort of problems a unit flying conventional jet aircraft would be likely to encounter if its airfield were attacked:

'The great thing to remember about any permanent airfield in Western Europe is that its position and its facilities will be very well known to the enemy. To imagine otherwise would be quite unrealistic. That means enemy pilots can pre-plan their attacks and make themselves familiar with the aiming points before they take off. Obviously, the easiest way to prevent operations by conventional jet aircraft is to attack their airfields and blow holes in the taxiways and runways in vital places. If the taxiways are cut, aircraft may be unable to get from their hardened shelters to the runway. And if they do, there may not be a sufficient length of runway clear of holes for the aircraft to take off. The attacking aircraft might also drop mines to disrupt repair work, and the taxiways and runway would have to be cleared of these before aircraft could move. That could be a lengthy business. Aircraft could be stuck in their shelters at the very time when they were desperately needed to support the land battle.'

For take-off or landing, conventional jet aircraft have only one operating option, and that involves the use of a long runway or other hardened concrete surface. If they are denied such a

(1) Air Marshall Sir Patrick Hine, Royal Air Force, Commander in Chief of the 2nd Allied Tactical Air Force, made up of units of the U.S., British, German, Belgian and Dutch Air Forces.

(2) Colonel Keith Robson of the British Army, who served on the staff of Headquarters Northern Army Group where he was responsible for co-ordinating air operations with those on land.

(3) Boeing E-3A Sentry AWACS aircraft, one of eighteen operated by the NATO Airborne Early Warning Force, based at Geilenkirchen in Germany. During any conflict in Europe these aircraft would play an important role in the tracking and interception of low-flying enemy aircraft.

(24) A pair of A-10 armoured close air support aircraft of the 509th Tactical Fighter Squadron USAF, based at Bentwaters in England. Each aircraft carries two Maverick electro-optically guided missiles on each inner-wing pylon, and a radar jamming pod on the port outer pylon. The multiple barrels of the 30mm armour-piercing cannon can be seen beneath the extreme nose of the aircraft.

(25) Lieutenant Colonel Tom Lyon, commander of the 509th Tactical Fighter Squadron.

(22) A Harrier of No. 3 Squadron Royal Air Force, moving into a camouflaged hide at field operating site in Germany, after a sortie.

(23) Dick Johns, pictured when he held the rank of Group Captain and commanded the Royal Air Force Germany Harrier Wing, comprising Nos. 3 and 4 Squadrons, normally based at Guetersloh.

(19, 20, 21) Test firing of MW-1 anti-tank munitions from the sides of the container under the fuselage of the Tornado. Once it is well clear of the aircraft, each of the clusters shown breaks up to release seven armour-piercing bomblets like the one inset (21); in this way the load of about 4,500 bomblets is spread evenly over an area twice as long and twice as wide as a football field, with a density sufficient to score hits on a high proportion of the vehicles in that area.

(18) Oberstleutnant Walter Jertz, operational commander of Jagdbombergeschwader 31.

(16) JP233 cratering bombs hitting a runway during a test of the system. As one bomb explodes to crater the runway the flash illuminates another descending on its retarding parachute.

(17) Tornado of Jagdbombergeschwader 31, German Air Force, based at Nörvenich in Germany. The aircraft carries a typical war load: MW-1 container under the fuselage, a Sidewinder missile on the side of each inner wing pylon, a chaff and flare dispensing pod on the port outer pylon and a radar-jamming pod on the starboard outer pylon. For normal operations these aircraft would carry a fuel tank under each inner-wing pylon, but the tanks would have to be jettisoned before MW-1 munitions could be fired from the aircraft.

(14) RAF Tornado releasing JP233 mines and runway cratering bombs during a test.

(15) View of the underside of the Tornado after the release of the JP233 munitions. The thirty runway cratering bombs had been stowed in the rear of each container and the 215 mines in the front section.

(12) Tornado GR 1 tactical attack bomber of No. 17 Squadron Royal Air Force, based at Brüggen in Germany.

(13) Wing Commander Grant McLeod, commander of No. 17 Squadron.

(10) F-111F tactical attack bomber of the 494th Tactical Fighter Squadron USAF, based at Lakenheath in England. The aircraft carries a typical war load of four 2,000 lb Paveway laser-guided bombs under the wings. The Pave Tack laser designator pod is under the centre fuselage and has the sighting head lowered. Behind the Pave Tack the aircraft carries a radar-jamming pod.

(11) Lieutenant-Colonel Paul Fazackerley, commander of the 494th Tactical Fighter Squadron.

(8) F-111E tactical attack bombers of the 79th Tactical Fighter Squadron USAF, over their base at Upper Heyford in England. Each aircraft carries eight 500 lb free-fall bombs on the wing pylons. In the background can be seen the dispersed and hardened shelters for the aircraft.

(9) Lieutenant-Colonel Peter Granger, commander of the 79th Tactical Fighter Squadron.

(6) F-4K Phantom air defence fighter of No. 92 Squadron Royal Air Force, outside a hardened air-craft shelter at its base at Wildenrath in Germany.

(7) F-16 Fighting Falcons of No. 311 Squadron Royal Netherlands Air Force, based at Volkel in Holland. These fighter-bombers can operate in the air defence or the attack roles, and are seen here equipped for the former, each carrying two Sidewinder missiles.

(4) F-15C Eagle air defence fighters of the 32nd Tactical Fighter Squadron USAF, based at Soesterberg in Holland.

(5) Major Charles Casey, Operations Officer of the 32nd Tactical Fighter Squadron.

(26) RF-4C Phantom reconnaissance aircraft of the 1st Tactical Reconnaissance Squadron USAF, based at Alconbury in England. In addition to optical and infra-red cameras this aircraft carries a TEREC electronic reconnaissance sensor, and a Pave Tack pod under the centre fuselage.

(27) Lieutenant-Colonel Carl Loveland, commander of the 1st Tactical Reconnaissance Squadron.

(28) Jaguar reconnaissance aircraft of No. 2 Squadron Royal Air Force, based at Laarbruch in Germany. The optical cameras and infra-red linescan system are housed in the pod under the fuselage.

(29) F-16 Fighting Falcon reconnaissance aircraft of No. 306 Squadron Royal Netherlands Air Force, based at Volkel in Holland, carrying a camera pod under the fuselage and Sidewinder missiles on the wing tips.

(30) Lynx anti-tank helicopter flying 'nap of the earth.' Four container-launchers for TOW anti-tank missiles are carried on each side of the fuselage. The missiles are tracked in flight using the periscopic binocular sighting head on top of the cabin.

(31) Lynx launching a TOW anti-tank guided missile from a typical firing position: in the hover with as little of the helicopter as possible showing above cover in the direction of the target.

(32) Gazelle light helicopter, used for battlefield reconnaissance role by British Army anti-tank helicopter squadrons.

(33) Lieutenant-Colonel Wilfred Hyde-Smith, British Army Air Corps, pictured when he was commander of No. 652 Squadron equipped with Lynx and Gazelle helicopters.

(34) EF-111 Raven radar-jamming aircraft of the 42nd Electronic Combat Squadron USAF, based at Upper Heyford in England.

(35) Lieutenant-Colonel David Vesely, commander of the 42nd Electronic Combat Squadron.

(36) F-4G Phantom 'Wild Weasel' aircraft of the 52nd Tactical Fighter Wing USAF, based at Spangdahlem in Germany. This unit specializes in operations against enemy radars and surface-to-air missile batteries, and the aircraft carries Shrike anti-radar missiles on the inner-wing pylons.

(37) Lieutenant-Colonel Les Kersey, Assistant Director of Operations of the 52nd Tactical Fighter Wing.

(38) Tornado of Marine Flieger Geschwader 1 of the German Navy, based at Jagel in Germany. The aircraft is fitted with a typical load for the anti-shipping role; two Kormoran radar homing air-to-surface missiles under the fuselage, a Sidewinder air-to-air missile for self-defence and a fuel tank on each inner-wing pylon, a radar-jamming pod under the starboard outer pylon and (out of sight on the other side of the aircraft) a chaff and flare dispensing pod on the port outer pylon.

(39) Fregattenkapitaen Volke Liche, Operational Commander of Marine Flieger Geschwader 1.

(40) German Navy Tornado launching a Kormoran during a test of the missile.

(41) Moment of impact of a Kormoran sea-skimming missile during a test firing against a decommissioned destroyer.

(42) A Tornado F2 interceptor of the Royal Air Force in its element, operating far out to sea in the defense of the United Kingdom.

(43) Air Vice Marshal Ken Hayr, commander of No. 11 Group Royal Air Force, responsible for the air defence of the United Kingdom and the surrounding waters.

(44) *Above:* Alphajet light attack aircraft of the German Air Force; the aircraft shown are equipped for the anti-helicopter role with a single 27mm cannon in a pod under the centre fuselage.

(45) *Below:* NF-5 light attack aircraft of No. 316 Squadron Royal Netherlands Air Force, based at Gilze-Rijen in Holland.

(46) *Below:* Mirage 5 light attack aircraft of the Belgian Air Force, with a pair of BL755 cluster bombs under the centre fuselage.

surface or access to one, the aircraft are tied to the ground.

In contrast, units flying Harriers have a whole range of operating options which mean that air attacks on their bases are most unlikely to prevent more than a small part of the force from flying attack missions:

'The Harrier allows a commander a whole range of operating options. First, if for some reason there is insufficient time for the force to move off-base, it can fight from its peacetime airfield. At Gütersloh the Harriers could sit out an attack in their hardened shelters. After the attack the Harriers would not need a prepared concrete strip to take off. At Gütersloh there are stretches of road and grass areas from which aircraft could operate if the runway and taxiways were blocked.

Before going any further I would stress that although the Harrier is able to take off vertically, it cannot do so carrying a full war load. It needs to take a short run to get off fully loaded. Because of this in Germany the Harrier is normally operated in the STOVL [short take off, vertical landing] mode.'

The need for a lengthened take-off run when carrying a load is not unique to the Harrier: *all* fixed-wing aircraft need a longer take-off run when heavily loaded. In fact the run needed by most conventional combat aircraft in this condition is between four and six times longer than that for a Harrier. In the case of the Harrier, moreover, the ability to 'air taxi' means that if it does not have a strip of sufficient length to hand, it can easily move to one, however pitted the ground in between:

'If, to take an extreme case, one of the squadron's dispersal areas was cratered to such an extent that even Harriers could not take off with normal loads, the aircraft would be unloaded and defuelled and do what we call an 'air taxi': vertical lift off and fly slowly like a helicopter to a part of the airfield where there was little or no damage, and land vertically there. Then the Harriers would be reloaded with fuel and bombs, and fly missions in the normal way. When Harriers return from their missions they have the capability – unique for a high-speed

aircraft – to land vertically each very close to its assigned
hardened shelter.

So, flying from a normal airfield, the Harrier's unique
capabilities give it a far wider range of operating options than
are possible for conventional jet aircraft. To crater an airfield
to the extent that Harriers could not operate would require a
density of attack out of all proportion to the military results
achieved.

Typical Harrier force dispersal

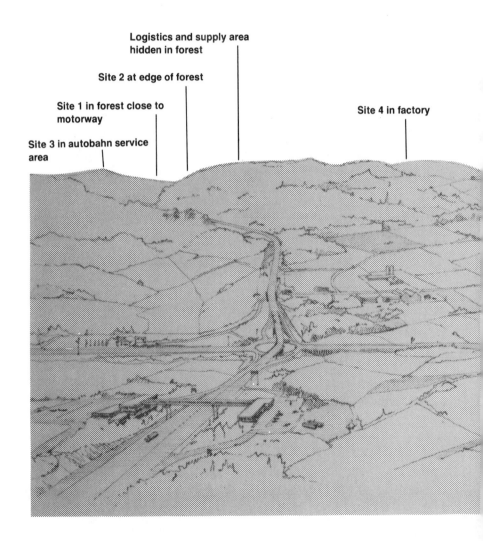

**Logistics and supply area
hidden in forest**

Site 2 at edge of forest

**Site 1 in forest close to
motorway**

Site 4 in factory

**Site 3 in autobahn service
area**

To prevent the Harrier force getting a sizeable proportion of its aircraft into the air would require a massive attack, which would have to be repeated at frequent intervals to prevent the minimal repair work necessary to enable Harriers to air-taxi to safer areas.

So much for the ability of the Harrier to operate from normal airfields after they had been attacked. But prevention is better than cure, and it is better to avoid being attacked in the first

Logistics and supply area at farm, using barns etc. for concealment

Site 6 at sports centre

Forward Wing Operations Centre in timberyard

Site 5 at out-of-town superstore

Logistics and supply area in town centre bus station

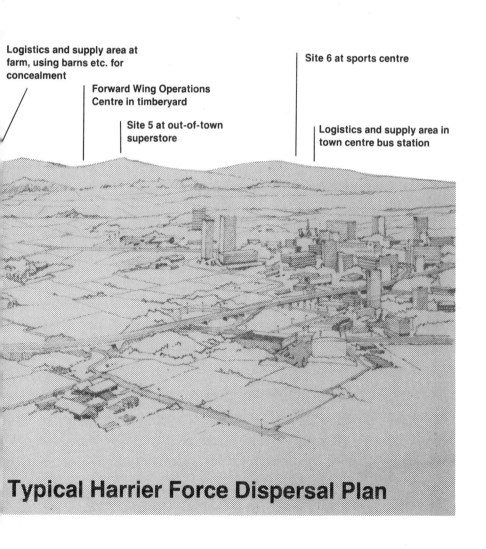

Typical Harrier Force Dispersal Plan

place. As everybody knows, the Harrier can operate from small camouflaged sites away from normal airfields. Dick Johns explained the rationale for this type of operation:

'It is most unlikely that any war in Europe could start with absolutely no warning. Almost certainly there would be a period beforehand when intelligence information told us that the enemy was preparing to attack. Of course we hope it never happens, but it is a possibility and it is our job to deter such a thing. During this warning time we could move the entire Harrier force off base and so achieve a much higher degree of protection through dispersal and concealment.'

When it moves into the field, the Harrier force is split between a number of camouflaged operating sites, each with its own aircraft maintenance, communications and administrative personnel. Every man, from the commander down, is armed and trained in basic infantry skills to defend the site if it comes under attack from the ground. In addition, protecting the general area around the sites, there would usually be an RAF Regiment unit with light tanks and armoured personnel carriers:

'When it moves off-base the Harrier force has to be self-sufficient in engineering support, still able to do major work such as aircraft engine changes or battle damage repairs to large components. To support Harriers in the field there would be what we call logistics parks holding fuel, ammunition and bombs together with heavy engineering kit, a full range of spares for the aircraft and specialized teams of engineers. Like the operating sites, the logistics parks would be carefully camouflaged and well away from the base airfield.

All this greatly reduces the scope for effective air attack by the enemy. The Harriers would not be operating from a known location, and the enemy would have to find each site before he could attack it. Even if he could pinpoint the location of a Harrier site exactly, its surroundings would be unfamiliar to the pilots of attacking aircraft. So dispersing the force would give an enemy two major problems: first, that of locating the Harrier sites: and second, that of attacking the small, indistinct targets that would be difficult for attack aircraft to find. And even if a Harrier site was found and hit hard, only a small proportion of the force would be affected. Aircraft airborne at the time of the attack would be diverted to other sites in the area. The damaged site would be abandoned and the surviving personnel, equipment, stores and ordnance loaded on trucks and taken to a different site – the plan is always to have spare sites prepared and ready for operations, in case of such an eventuality.'

The big advantage of using concealed sites is that Harriers can survive while operating far closer to the front line – and the troops they are to support – than is possible for conventional jet attack aircraft tied to concrete runways. Because of this the Harrier attack missions are likely to be short, the aircraft would not normally need to carry underwing fuel tanks, and so all five mounting points could be used to carry weapons. It also means that Harriers would be able to react to demands for air support much more quickly than any other type of high-speed attack aircraft:

'Being closer to the battle line gives a short reaction time. When Harriers are given a job to do they can get to the scene of action much faster than conventional aircraft coming from the main clutch of airfields further to the west. So at normal cruising speeds they are much closer to the battle. And because the Harrier force has direct communications with the army corps headquarters to which it is allocated, reaction time is reduced still further.'

When sending attack aircraft into action with conventional weapons, it is important that the force dispatched be sufficiently large to hit the enemy really hard. Otherwise it is probably not worth the effort of mounting the attack in the first place. Normally attack Harriers would operate in pairs, and for a large attack several pairs would be sent in close succession against the target:

'I don't believe in sending Harriers to attack in penny

packets. I'm dead against that, it's dispersing one's effort. If one sends attack aircraft a pair here and a pair there, that is delivering pinpricks. It may annoy the enemy but it is not going to have any telling effect on the land–air battle.

The great thing about air power is the ability to concentrate devastating force rapidly at great distances from base, and use it to hit a target of major importance to the enemy. In a war in Central Europe I would expect that a high proportion of the Harrier attack sorties would be mounted in forces of twelve aircraft or more.

I have always looked at the Harrier force as a sledgehammer. If, say, twenty-four aircraft suddenly and unexpectedly put down over a hundred cluster bombs in a space of about two minutes on a concentration of enemy armour caught on a

Harrier urban deployment site. In wartime the Harrier would often operate from urban sites, which offer a good basic infrastructure of roads and facilities. Cover is frequently available, and hardened areas for take-offs and landings are plentiful. Supermarkets make excellent hides, once their plate-glass frontages have been disposed of, and their car parks can make useful mini-airstrips

road and unable to deploy tactically, that would certainly be a telling blow. The enemy troops would not be keen to be on the receiving end of another dose like that. And you have to consider not only the direct killing effect of the bombs, but their psychological impact as well. It could even be that the attack put out of action the regimental commander and some of his staff; given the rigid command structure used by the Soviets, that could certainly cause problems to a unit preparing to go into the attack. Once such an target had been found and attacked, the Harriers could mount repeat sorties into the area as needed.'

In this context it should of course be stressed that the Harrier force would not be operating alone. Although the Harriers would probably be the first to reach and attack a concentration of vehicles found in the enemy rear area, if the target was considered important to the land battle scores of other attack aircraft would follow from bases further back.

Dick Johns then discussed the sort of battlefield air interdiction targets against which he thought the Harrier would be most effective:

'In my view the job the Harrier would be best at is attacking targets on the far side of the battle line. The sort of target I have in mind is a concentration of enemy tanks and vehicles which, by definition, would be much easier to find from the air than a single small target. In a large-scale action on land one can imagine many instances when suitable targets would appear. For example, if the forward element of an enemy attack had been fought to a standstill by our troops, the enemy commander would move up reinforcements to regain the impetus of his attack. We would be looking for natural barricades where the enemy could be held up, like a river or a mined road where vehicles could become cramped together; or a valley where they could not get off the road to disperse; or a river crossing where vehicles were queuing up to go across. Those would be excellent places to hit them.

The Harrier force would try to find and attack vehicles which had not deployed tactically off the roads and dispersed into fields, because dispersed vehicles are much more difficult to find and hit from the air. Bearing in mind the threat to them from our own artillery, I would expect the enemy vehicles all to be deployed tactically by the time they reached a point 5 to 10 kilometres before our troops' forward positions. So the preferred killing area for the Harriers would be in the strip of land between about 10 and 30 kilometres behind the front line. That far back there would be no problems of identification, and any military vehicle seen could be treated as hostile.

Because they can be based close to the front line and do not need to go a long way to reach their targets, Harriers can zip back and forth between their forward base and the target at a high rate. It is perfectly feasible to fly what we call a 'half hour cycle', say take off at 9 o'clock, land at 9.30, refuel and rearm, take off again at 10, land at 10.30 and so on as long as the aeroplane stays serviceable. Usually the pilot would remain in the cockpit between sorties. Obviously, the greater the number of sorties flown the greater the damage the Harrier force could inflict on the enemy.'

Dick Johns was less keen about using the Harrier in the close air support role, against targets in the vicinity of friendly troops:

'Given the amount of smoke and dust likely to be over the battle area, in my view there is a danger in this sort of operation that fast attack aircraft could do as much damage to friendly troops as to the enemy. That is simply a fact of life. So I would not want Harriers involved in that sort of battle except as a last resort or in exceptional circumstances. In my view the Harrier is not really a close air support aeroplane. It can do the job, but there are risks inherent in such an operation.'

The discussion then shifted to the second of the Harrier's main roles in Germany, tactical reconnaissance. Harriers engaged in reconnaissance missions in the battle area would fly singly. One of the Harrier force squadrons, No. 4, has the dual roles of tactical reconnaissance and ground attack. For reconnaissance the aircraft have a built-in port-facing camera or, if horizon-to-horizon photography is required, a reconnaissance pod is mounted under the fuselage. When the squadron deploys from Gütersloh it would take with it a mobile reconnaissance intelligence centre with facilities for the rapid processing and interpretation of aerial photographs. No. 3 Squadron's aircraft have a limited photographic reconnaissance capability using the built-in camera. All Harrier pilots are trained in photographic and visual reconnaissance techniques.

'During reconnaissance missions Harrier pilots would try to report by radio anything of vital interest that they saw. A pilot might report seeing a long column of enemy tanks and other vehicles moving along the road in such and such a position. This information would immediately be passed to army corps headquarters. About half an hour after landing, the films from the cameras would have been developed and the photo interpreters, working from negatives to save the time of printing, would be able to identify specific types of vehicle and from that deduce the type of unit seen, say the headquarters element of a motor-rifle division.'

Normally the RAF Harriers in Germany would stick to their assigned roles of ground attack and reconnaissance, and not seek combat with enemy aircraft in the air. But if they were cornered by enemy fighters and had to fight back there is no doubt the jump jets would prove mean little adversaries. Any reference to air-to-air combat must include mention of the Harrier's unique ability of use VIFF (thrust vectored in forward flight), though Dick Johns felt it would not be a significant factor during low-level operations over Germany:

'A lot of rubbish has been talked about VIFFing. A pilot might use VIFF to bring his guns or missiles to bear on an enemy aircraft, by changing the angle of sight very quickly over relatively short arcs. That is an offensive application of VIFF. But by and large its merits are defensive rather than offensive. The real advantage VIFF can bring is when a Harrier is threatened and needs to turn or decelerate rapidly to escape. Or if an infra-red homing missile has been launched at the Harrier from the ground or the air, then the pilot might use VIFF to angle the Harrier away from the missile and deflect the infra-red energy away from the aeroplane. Another great advantage of having the ability to VIFF – even if it is not used – is that opposing pilots will know the aircraft is able to perform in unpredictable ways and this would make them reluctant to get into a dogfight with a Harrier.

In any future conflict a proportion of the attack or reconnaissance Harriers would carry Sidewinder air-to-air missiles for self-defence. That should make enemy fighter pilots even more cautious about attacking them. An enemy pilot would not know which Harriers were 'Stingers', aircraft carrying Sidewinders, and which were not. It would be a brave or a very foolhardy man who did not consider that any Harrier he saw was likely to be a 'Stinger', and treat them all with respect. If I was an enemy fighter pilot trying to engage a Harrier formation the uncertainty would worry me, not knowing which Harriers had the capability to nail me if I made a mistake. If a 'Stinger' came under attack from an enemy fighter there would be a lot of things the Harrier pilot could do to force the enemy into an overtaking position, and once the enemy aircraft was in front it could have a Sidewinder streaking after it.'

Dick Johns ended with a review of the lessons from the Falklands conflict, as they might apply to operations in Germany:

'The conflict proved what we had always supposed, that the Harrier is very rugged, able to take a lot of battle damage and still get home. That was most reassuring. The Harrier had a significant impact on the conduct of a land battle, though I think one should be careful not to read across the wrong lessons for a possible future conflict in Central Europe. Over the Falklands the RAF Harriers operated in small units, with no interference from enemy fighters, and were, by and large, safe from ground defences except in the immediate area around targets. It would not be like that in any war in Central Europe.

I was particularly impressed by the operation in which four reinforcement Harriers flew direct from Ascension Island to HMS *Hermes* off the Falklands, in 8½-hour flights covering some 3,300 nautical miles. It was yet another demonstration of the enormous mobility that is possible with air power, that we could get a small aircraft like the Harrier down there in one hop using in-flight refuelling. Of course, there were risks involved. Had anything serious gone wrong with an aircraft during the flights, its pilot's chances of survival would have been minimal. But nothing did go wrong. The pilots – none of whom had landed a Harrier on a carrier before – flew the operation perfectly. And within a few hours those aircraft were ready to go into action. I think it was a tremendous feat of stamina, cold courage, and a ready acceptance of risks which speaks volumes for the calibre of the people we have flying these aeroplanes. And it says a lot for their training.

I think the most important tactical lesson to come out of the conflict is the need for attack aircraft to deliver their bombs and rockets from altitudes even lower than we had previously used, if they are to survive in highly defended areas. We have altered our training schedules, and now pilots release bombs from lower altitudes and at significantly greater speeds than previously. But by and large the training given to Harrier pilots, and the tactics they used, stood them in good stead over the South Atlantic. We have not seen any need to make major changes there, and that too was very reassuring.'

9: The Battlefield Bruisers

Lieutenant-Colonel Tom Lyon joined the US Air Force in 1968. After pilot training he was assigned to the 602nd Tactical Fighter Squadron in Thailand, flying A-1 Skyraider attack aircraft in support of rescue helicopters operating over Vietnam, Cambodia and Laos. On his return to the USA he instructed A-1 pilots, then flew A-7 attack aircraft with the 23rd Tactical Fighter Wing. Between 1978 and 1980 he instructed at the A-10 conversion school at Tucson, Arizona. After a year at Staff College he was posted to Headquarters 4th Tactical Air Force at Heidelberg in Germany as an air operations staff officer. In August 1983 he was posted to Bentwaters in England and the following year assumed command of the 509th Tactical Fighter Squadron flying A-10s.

The 509th Tactical Fighter Squadron is one of six Fairchild A-10 Thunderbolt squadrons, each with an establishment of eighteen aircraft and thirty-four pilots, based at Bentwaters and Wood-bridge in eastern England. The A-10 is a single-seat twin-engined armoured attack aircraft specially built for the close air support role; as currently equipped it would normally operate only by day. In the combat configuration the A-10 takes off at a weight of about 15 tons, and its maximum speed at low altitude is about 325 knots.

In time of tension the 509th and the two other A-10 squadrons assigned to 2 ATAF would move from their peacetime bases in England to forward operating bases in northern Germany. Among the airfields in the 2 ATAF area earmarked for A-10s are Ahlorn near Bremen and Nörvenich near Cologne.

Not even the most devoted supporter of the A-10 would say it is a beautiful aircraft. But the ungainly machine lacks the graceful contours of its faster cousins for a good reason: the A-10 is built to withstand severe punishment as well as dish it out:

'The A-10 is the only NATO airplane designed and built specifically to defeat enemy armour. Its dedicated role is to mount close air support and shallow battlefield air interdiction missions, in support of our ground forces. The A-10 incorporates many of the lessons the US Air Force learned during ground attack operations over Korea and Vietnam, and during its design a lot of thought went into ways of enabling it to survive battle damage.'

To help .it avoid hits from radar-laid anti-aircraft fire and infra-red homing missiles, the A-10 is fitted with an ALQ-119 radar jamming pod, an ALR-69 radar homing and warning receiver and ALE-40 dispensers for chaff and infra-red decoy flares. Yet, such is the volume of enemy fire likely to be aimed at it in the battle area, the aircraft is almost certain to take some hits. The A-10 has been designed to survive hits by rounds from small-calibre automatic guns and lightweight anti-aircraft missiles, the sort of weapons it would encounter during operations over enemy front-line troops. Where possible, those parts of the aircraft which are vulnerable to battle damage have been protected or duplicated. The pilot sits under a canopy of thick toughened glass while beneath him is an armoured 'bathtub' of titanium thick enough to withstand hits from 23 mm rounds. The aircraft's two engines are mounted in separate pods with separate fuel systems, so that if one is shot out the other will continue working. The fuel tanks are filled with fire-retardant foam and are self-sealing: if a bullet pierces the side of a tank and fuel starts to leak out, the hole will seal itself automatically. The flying controls are hydraulically operated, but there is a secondary manual back-up system. Moreover, if battle damage causes a rudder, an aileron or an elevator to jam, in each case the remaining one is designed to continue working independently, allowing the pilot sufficient control to get home and land. If the undercarriage hydraulic system is damaged and the wheels will not extend normally, the pilot has an emergency system to allow the wheels to drop out of their housings under gravity, then the airflow will push the legs back and down and lock them in place.

These and other design features enable the A-10 to continue operating after damage which would send most other types of aircraft cartwheeling out of control.

The faster types of attack aircraft rely on their speed to survive over enemy territory. But to enable it to do its job properly the A-10 was specifically designed for relatively low-speed operations:

'Compared with other jet aircraft the A-10 is not fast: fully loaded at low altitude its maximum speed is about 325 knots. But to see and attack individual enemy armoured vehicles in the battle area close to our own troops you need to fly fairly slowly. We have to be able to identify our targets positively before each firing pass or there would be a serious risk of hitting friendly forces.'

The primary anti-tank weapon carried by the A-10 is the 30 mm cannon. The aircraft was literally built around its GAU-8 seven-barrelled Gatling gun, which fires projectiles weighing just under a pound at a muzzle velocity of 3,240 feet per second and at a rate of 4,200 per minute. Complete with drum magazine holding 1,174 rounds of ammunition, this huge weapon is nearly 20 feet long and weighs just over 4,000 lb.

'The gun has a maximum effective range of about 6,000 feet and is our main weapon. The armour-piercing round we use against tanks has an aluminum shell inside which is a 'penetrator' of heavy metal. This penetrator is about four inches long and the thickness of a pencil, and has a mass somewhat greater than lead. When the shell hits a tank at high velocity the aluminum shell breaks away and the penetrator continues on through the armour like a nail through wood. As it passes through armour the penetrator will generate enormous heat, enough to kill or incapacitate the tank's crew, and it breaks off chunks of armour which split away at high velocity, causing further damage inside the vehicle.'

Supplementing its cannon the A-10 will normally carry two,

four or six Maverick guided missiles on underwing racks. At launch this missile weighs 462 lb, of which 130 lb is a shaped-charge warhead able to penetrate the armour of any known tank. The Maverick employs electro-optical guidance and is fitted with a TV camera in its nose. Before he launches the missile the A-10 pilot is able to see on a screen in his cockpit the picture of the ground in front of the aircraft, coming from the TV camera of the Maverick he has selected. The pilot moves a control on his throttle to place an aiming cross over the target he wishes to engage, thereby locking-on the missile to an image contrast: a dark target against a light background or a light target against a dark background:

'Maverick is a 'launch-and-leave' weapon: if we can see a tank we can lock on a Maverick, push the button, and the Maverick will launch and home on the target. Once it is on its way we don't have to do anything else, we can evade or engage the next target.'

Other weapons that could be carried by the A-10 include Rockeye anti-armour cluster bombs and retarded or non-retarded 500 lb bombs. These types of free-fall bomb are considerably less accurate than the aircraft's primary anti-tank weapons, however, and to use them the A-10 would have to fly over or very close to its target with the resultant danger that would entail.

Normally A-10's operate in pairs, with sometimes two pairs coming together to deliver a co-ordinated attack on an enemy armoured force. The aircraft would approach the battle area at ultra-low altitude making maximum possible use of ground cover. Since their primary mission is close air support against enemy forces in the vicinity of friendly troops, the A-10s would be directed on to precise targets found for them by forward air controllers on the ground or in helicopters.

For a typical attack with Maverick a pair of A-10s would climb rapidly over friendly territory to 1,000 feet or until their target was in view, whichever was the lower. If the forward air controller was designating the target with a laser, the laser receiver equipment in the nose of the A-10 would pick up the energy reflected from the target and convert it into direction-to-steer signals on the head-up display in front of the pilot:

'Remembering the defences the A-10 could encounter, if visibility was good enough we would try to engage the targets with Mavericks from long range; if we could climb to about 1,000 feet and are able to lock-on Mavericks at two miles we can fire one or two from there and return to cover, without going within range of the guns defending the target. However, the problem with Maverick over Central Europe is that for much of the time the visibility is not good enough to use it. If the pilot cannot see the target on his TV screen he cannot lock-on a Maverick, and would have to go in closer and use the gun.'

The optimum firing range for the A-10's 30 mm cannon is between 4,000 and 6,000 feet (¾ mile and just over 1 mile), and because the aircraft is now much closer to the enemy a somewhat more agile type of attack is necessary:

'For a gun attack we would do a rapid climb to about 700 feet, the whole time in a continually varying turn to make things as difficult as possible for enemy gunners trying to shoot at us. With its large wing the A-10 has excellent manoeuvrability. At the top of the climb we would bank into a five-degree descent, line up on the target, level the wings and fire a one-second burst – thirty or forty rounds. Just one round penetrating the armour of a tank will give a high probability of a kill, so a longer burst would only waste bullets. And the gun's recoil causes so much vibration that one cannot hold the gun to the target for any longer than that. After firing we would go back into the turn; once we were exposed to enemy fire it would be important not to fly in a straight line for more than five seconds.'

If enemy tanks were close together it might be possible to realign the cannon on a second target and loose off a burst at it too, before the requirements of survival forced the A-10 to return to cover close to the ground:

'To maximize the effect of the plane and its gun, the more fire power we can bring to bear on a collection of armoured vehicles the better. We would try to set up a cycle of attacks: a pair of A-10s would make their attack, as they pulled away a second pair would go in to attack from a different direction, then shortly afterwards the first pair would return to make a further attack from another still, and so on. Each new attack would be launched from a direction different from the one before to maintain the confusion for the other side.

If we found a large concentration of enemy tanks we would send in pairs of A-10s in relays to work them over. We would spread our attacks over a long period, so that pairs of aircraft would return to base at intervals and our ground crews could concentrate their efforts to turn them around rapidly and get them back into the air. The more aircraft we could keep airborne at any time, the less would be left on the ground and vulnerable to enemy air attack. We would not send off, say, sixteen aircraft in one go, because after they had expended their munitions they would all come back to the airfield at the same time and it would be a long time before we could get them back into action.'

Over Central Europe it is normally considered too hazardous for fast jets to make a second attack run over their target once the defences have been alerted; these aircraft would release all their bombs or rockets during a single pass and then go home. But in the area close to the land battle the enemy anti-aircraft defences would be considerably less lethal than those around targets further back. It has never been proved in action, but Tom Lyon believes that this difference would enable the heavily armoured A-10s to continue attacking until their fuel or munitions ran out or there were no targets left:

'Repeat attacks would be part of our day-to-day business, though not repeat attacks in the sense of pulling off after hitting one tank, turning round and going back immediately to hit another. We would leave the area and attack the same group of tanks from a different direction two or three minutes later. In my opinion an A-10 should be able to hit ten tanks

during a single mission. It carries enough ammunition and
enough Mavericks to do that.

Fast jets like Harriers would make one attack on a target,
release all their bombs and be away. They would not make
multiple passes, and rightly so. So it would take them ten or
twelve planes to put in a good attack on a concentration of
vehicles, making one pass with each of them. I would take two
or four A-10s and make twenty passes, making more firing
passes with fewer planes.'

Tom Lyon regards the A-10s as complementary to the fast-jet
attack aircraft, not in competition with them. Although the A-10
is an excellent aircraft for the close air support role, its survival
depends on its not going far beyond the enemy front-line troops.
Troop movements further back would be defended by heavier
mobile air defence missile systems such as the SA-4, SA-6 and
SA-8, and a hit from any of these weapons would demolish an
A-10 despite its armour. For this reason the large concentrations
of enemy vehicles moving along roads to the battle area, the sort
of target sought after by the fast jets, are not really suitable for
the A-10s:

'Convoys are something the faster jets can look after. If an
A-10 pilot sees one he is in serious trouble; he should not go
that deep into enemy territory because it would be difficult for
our airplane to survive there. The further past the battle area
they send me, the more unhappy I am going to be.

In a war there would be plenty of targets for everyone. I
think the various types of battlefield support aircraft comple-
ment each other very well. Look across the spectrum of
aircraft we have: F-111s and Tornadoes doing their deep
interdiction against bridges and fixed targets; the F-16s,
Harriers and other shorter-range attack aircraft hitting targets
behind the battle area; then the A-10s and attack helicopters
hitting tanks close to our own troops in the actual battle area.
Our battlefield support effort has to be seen as a whole.'

Tom Lyon outlined what he considered to be the main threats
to A-10s operating in the battle area:

'Over the battlefield the biggest threat to us is from mobile anti-aircraft gun systems like the Soviet 23 mm ZSU 23-4, which can be deployed close to their forward troops. So we tell our forward air controllers, 'You locate the enemy air defence systems for us, let us take those out first, then we can go in and hit the tanks.' If air defence systems like the ZSU 23-4 are tactically deployed to give a good field of fire, they have to be in the open where we can find them. We expect to be able to spot, take on and destroy those systems first. If visibility was good enough we would engage them with Maverick, if not we would stand off at 6,000 feet outside their effective range and hit them with the gun. Compared with tanks they are thin-skinned vehicles; our 30 mm rounds would go through them like a hot knife through butter.'

Of the air-to-air threats facing the A-10, Tom Lyon considered fighters to be low down on his list of worries:

'No enemy fighter can turn with us. If they try to attack us we would turn inside them, get into a firing position and open up at them with the GAU-8. When we fire the cannon it gives off a huge cloud of white smoke, so the enemy pilot would know we were shooting at him and that would certainly get his attention! A fighter pilot will tell you that any time the nose of an enemy plane carrying a weapon that could engage him is pointed in his direction, he should turn away. If he didn't and our 30 mm rounds hit his aircraft, they would tear it to pieces.

In my view a more serious airborne threat to us is the armed helicopter like the Hind with a 23 mm cannon. I can outgun him if I can see him far enough away, but a helicopter close to the ground is darned hard to see. During a firing run I would get only one chance to hit him. If I missed, or if I didn't see him in the first place and got too close to him, I could become the hunted. I don't like the odds. He can out-turn me, all he has to do is put his nose on me and I become a target for him. I respect the Hind, most A-10 pilots do.'

Because of their relatively long endurance and ability to carry out repeat attacks, the A-10s would orbit just behind the battle area waiting for suitable targets to become available. Similar 'cab rank' tactics were used by attack aircraft during the Second World War and the Korean War:

'We have been trying out ways of making best use of the A-10 against multiple armoured formations. In the past we were assigned a target, and if we had hit those tanks we were to go home even if we had fuel and ammunition left. Now if we had hit one target and had fuel and munitions remaining, we would wait at a holding area until another target was found for us.'

As well as mounting their own attacks on enemy armour, A-10s can co-ordinate their activities with those of anti-tank helicopters. Operating together, the two weapons systems can provide a deadly counter to enemy armoured formations which have broken through the main defensive line:

'Exercises have shown that A-10s and helicopters working together to launch co-ordinated attacks on enemy tanks would be more effective and suffer fewer losses than if either worked alone. We would operate in what is known as a 'joint air attack team' with US Army Cobra attack helicopters. The helicopters would locate the enemy armour and attack with TOW missiles; as they moved to new firing positions we would attack from a different direction, then the helicopters and ourselves would take it in turns to make repeated attacks with our different weapons.'

Based relatively close to the battle area and lacking the Harrier's ability to operate from concealed sites, the A-10 units have to expect their airfields to come under enemy air attack. Under such circumstances Tom Lyon believes the safest place for his aircraft would be in the air. As A-10s return to base to refuel and rearm they would go into their hardened shelters. If for any reason an A-10 unit was forced to leave its base it could go to another airfield or operate from straight lengths of autobahn. But the aircraft is too heavy to operate from fields:

'For all-weather operations the A-10 needs a 5,000-foot runway. We can also work from straight sections of autobahn. It is questionable whether we could work off dirt strips or grass; they would have to be very smooth and hard.'

Tom Lyon concluded by summing up the value of the A-10 in its highly specialized combat role:

'The A-10 is a simple plane to fly, it is forgiving and very reliable mechanically. But to get the most out of it demands a lot from the pilot; he has to work hard.

The A-10 is the only aircraft NATO has which was designed specifically for the close air support role and the destruction of enemy armour. It was designed for one thing and one thing only: to kill tanks and armoured vehicles. Our pilots specialize in that one role and they are very good at it. There is no aircraft in the world that can perform that mission better than the A-10.'

10: The Intelligence Gatherers

Lieutenant-Colonel Carl Loveland entered the US Air Force in 1970. After pilot training he joined his first squadron, the 62nd Tactical Reconnaissance Squadron flying RF-4 Phantoms at Shaw Air Force Base in South Carolina, in 1972. Between 1975 and 1978 he was posted as flight commander to the 1st Tactical Reconnaissance Squadron at Alconbury in England. In 1981 he was appointed to the Pentagon where he served two staff tours, the first in mission area analysis and the second as branch chief of air force reconnaissance plans dealing with current and future reconnaissance systems. In July 1984 he returned to England to take command of the 1st Tactical Reconnaissance Squadron.

The 1st Tactical Reconnaissance Squadron is based at Alconbury in England and is equipped with eighteen McDonnell Douglas RF-4C Phantoms. The RF-4C is the reconnaissance version of the Phantom fighter and is a twin-engined aircraft with a take-off weight of about 23 tons in the combat configuration. The RF-4C is equipped for night and all-weather operations and carries a crew of two, a pilot and a weapon systems officer. It is capable of supersonic speed at all altitudes but this increases the rate of fuel consumption considerably.

The nose of the RF-4C houses a battery of five optical cameras for low-altitude reconnaissance. One, the K-56, is fitted with a panoramic lens and is able to take single photographs of the ground extending from horizon to horizon on each side of the aircraft. The other four cameras are of the more conventional KS-87 type, arranged to cover the ground around the aircraft's forward hemisphere: one looks forward and slightly downwards from the extreme nose, one looks vertically downwards and the other two look out to each side and slightly downwards.

In the aft portion of the nose is an AAD-5 infra-red system, able to produce pictures at night that are almost as clear as the photographs from a normal camera in daylight. The system is completely passive; it makes no emissions that could be picked up by an enemy. The AAD-5 works on near-optical wavelengths and so is affected by smoke or haze in the vicinity of targets, though less so than normal optical cameras.

The Phantom's fan of optical cameras and the infra-red system enable it to record anything passing beneath it by day or night. But to use them effectively the aircraft would have to fly almost directly over the target and in wartime this could be a hazardous business. To enable its crew to observe targets from a distance, the RF-4C carries a Pave Tack pod under the fuselage. On the F-111F this pod is used to designate targets for laser-guided bombs, but on the RF-4C it is used in an entirely different way, as Carl Loveland explained:

'The Pave Tack pod carries an infra-red detecting set, like a television camera with a zoom lens, which the weapon systems officer can train by remote control to look at the area of interest. Both crewmen can view the Pave Tack pictures on the screens in front of them. Pave Tack enables us to see at night and gives a stand-off capability, allowing us to view defended targets from a distance without flying directly over them. From 30,000 feet Pave Tack allows us to view targets up to thirty miles away, by night or by day.'

Like the AAD-5, Pave Tack operates on near-optical infra-red wavelengths and cloud or industrial haze will reduce its range. And the television picture it gives is less sharp than those produced by the aircraft's optical or infra-red cameras. But despite these limitations Pave Tack is an extremely effective reconnaissance tool and its addition to the Phantom has added greatly to the aircraft's intelligence-gathering ability. A video-recorder in the pod records everything seen during the flight, for play-back and analysis after the aircraft has landed.

The other high-tech electronic reconnaissance sensor carried by the RF-4C is the TEREC (Tactical Electronic REConnaissance system). This is a passive receiver which can be programmed to search the radio frequency spectrum for signals from designated unfriendly radars. When their signals are detected

TEREC automatically sorts out the pulse trains from each and takes a series of running bearings on their sources. A micro-computer keeps track of the bearings thus found and, by a process of triangulation, works out the position of each one relative to the aircraft. The resultant information is recorded and stored within the equipment; it can be displayed on the screen in the weapon systems operator's cockpit and simultaneously re-transmitted to a ground station in friendly territory for further analysis:

'The sort of emitters we would use TEREC to locate would be, typically, the acquisition radars of a certain type of surface-to-air missile system. Obviously, a knowledge of the latest positions of an enemy's SAM batteries is of immense value to our attack aircraft, to enable them to route around the danger areas when flying to and from their targets. But, even more important, if we know where the enemy has concentrated his air defences that will tell us a great deal. An army moves its surface-to-air missile systems in conjunction with its ground troops. So if we see a certain pattern of air defence units we can get a good idea of the location of the troops they are defending.'

The RF-4C carries five optical cameras, an infra-red camera, a Pave Tack pod and a TEREC electronic reconnaissance system. Many of these sensors give overlapping capabilities and at first sight it might seem that the number carried is more than is strictly necessary. But Carl Loveland believes they are all needed:

'If you are going to risk your neck to look at a heavily defended target, you want to make sure you pick up every possible bit of information. You don't want to have to go back there again unless it is absolutely necessary . . .'

To enable it to survive at low altitude deep inside enemy territory the RF-4C carries an ALR-46 radar warning receiver, an ALQ-131 self-protection radar jamming pod and chaff and infra-red decoy flares. During operational missions the RF-4C would carry no weapons for self-protection, even though technically it would be a simple matter to modify it to carry air-to-air missiles. Carl Loveland explained the reasoning behind this:

'There are two schools of thought on whether to arm tactical reconnaissance aircraft with missiles for self-protection. Certainly a couple of Sidewinders would be very useful if the aircraft was cornered by enemy fighters. But in war reconnaissance is so important, and we have so few aircraft with which to do it, that we cannot allow those we have to be diverted from their primary job. In the past there have been many occasions when reconnaissance pilots flying aircraft carrying missiles have let themselves be diverted from their reconnaissance task, to go off and try to shoot down enemy aircraft. When the adrenalin starts to flow that sort of thing can happen . . . So the decision has been taken not to arm our tactical reconnaissance Phantoms.'

Having outlined the equipment carried by the RF-4C, Carl Loveland went on to describe its place in the overall reconnaissance-gathering capability of the NATO forces:

'A military commander needs to know what the enemy is doing; aerial reconnaissance will provide him with some of that information. There are several different systems and the RF-4C is only one of many. The full range includes satellites, short-range battlefield drones, very low flying aircraft and very high flying aircraft. Each system of collecting information – for that is what reconnaissance is – has unique applications. And each complements the others. To get the information he needs, a commander would use whichever system was most appropriate for the particular target.

RF-4C tactical reconnaissance missions would provide only a part – but a very important part – of the overall picture. We cannot sweep very large geographic areas taking photographs to gain information. The aircraft has the electronic 'eyes' and 'ears' to survey quite large areas, but our photographs can cover only specific areas of interest; instead of looking at a large area as one can with the naked eye, the area we photograph can be likened to what one sees looking down a soda straw – an area observed in very fine detail, but it is only a very small portion of the whole.'

Carl Loveland described some of the RF-4C's operating methods, starting with the intelligence it would seek to gather before an outbreak of hostilities:

'During a period of international tension we might find ourselves flying up and down the inner German border at 20,000 to 30,000 feet inside friendly territory, using TEREC and Pave Tack to keep an eye on what was happening the other side. If an enemy was preparing for war he would be moving troops and vehicles into forward positions. With them would go the various mobile air defence systems, which would probably have to be turned on and tested in the new positions. With our sensors we would be able to follow what they were doing, around the clock.'

Once fighting had started, the RF-4Cs would continue to gain much useful information by operating their advanced recon- naissance systems over friendly territory. But there would also be uses for these aircraft on the other side of the battle line:

'Another use of TEREC and Pave Tack would be during pre-strike reconnaissance missions. In that case we would go in between 5 and 15 minutes (40 and 120 miles) ahead of an attack formation to confirm the position of a moving target, for example an army unit advancing along a road. We would use Pave Tack to check that the target was where it was expected to be. If last-minute adjustments were required to the raid plan, we would radio these to the attack formation. As he neared the objective the weapon systems officer in the RF-4C would establish the locations of the air defence radars in the target area using TEREC, and pass these to the attack force as well.'

Another important role for the RF-4Cs in time of war, and one

for which they are particularly well-equipped, is the reconnaissance of enemy rear areas at night:

'Once hostilities open it is likely that most of the fighting will
take place by day, and most movement up to the battle area
will take place by night. A typical route reconnaissance task
would be to fly along a series of roads behind the battle area at
night using Pave Tack to look for large-scale movements of
vehicles, exploring the probable avenues of advance an enemy
ground force might use. After such movements had been
detected, or as soon as we regained friendly territory, we
would pass the information directly to the army command
post on UHF or HF radio. An army battle commander would
not need a glossy photograph of a long line of T.80 tanks
moving along a road to convince him that there was a Soviet
Guards tank division moving towards his part of the battle
area. What he would need would be rapid but accurate
information on what the enemy was doing, backed up later
with more detailed intelligence when the aircraft's films and
Pave Tack recording had been interpreted.'

A further very important wartime role for the RF-4C would be
post-attack reconnaissance:

'After an attack the air commander would need to know how
effectively the target had been hit. For example, an important
enemy military airfield might have fifty or more aircraft on it,
and if our attack aircraft had been able to knock out the
runway those aircraft would be unable to operate. After the
attack, reconnaissance aircraft would have to be sent in to
discover whether the runway was in fact closed. Pave Tack
would be very useful for this because it allows us to observe
targets from a distance without having to go within range of
the point defences around them. Again, that sort of information would be passed back by radio. The air commander
would need to know as soon as possible whether or not the
raid had been successful, and if another was necessary.
   At the end of the twelve hours, or soon after, a further
reconnaissance of the target would have to be flown to

determine the state of the repairs to the airfield, to help the commander decide when the next attack would be needed. Indeed, a single reconnaissance aircraft might be sent on a round trip to visit three or four targets which had been attacked, say airfields and bridges, to see if repairs had been completed to any. Or, if time and cloud conditions allowed, it might be possible for other reconnaissance systems – for example, satellites – to keep watch on such targets.'

In spite of the impressive capability of the stand-off reconnaissance systems carried by the RF-4C, there would be times when these aircraft would have to fly low over targets in enemy territory to take detailed photographs:

'The altitude at which we would fly during a photographic mission would depend on the strength of the defences confronting us. Typically, in a heavily defended area, an RF-4C would fly through the target area at 200 to 300 feet at speeds of up to 600 knots. On the other hand, if we were not being shot at, 'low altitude' might be as high as 2,000 or 3,000 feet to give the greatest area of coverage for our optical and infra-red cameras.

During photographic missions we would switch on our cameras only in the target areas. We would not want to expose vast amounts of film on the way to and from the target, which would probably gather little extra information but would swamp our photographic interpretation organization with more material than they could handle.

For the majority of targets the RF-4Cs would fly alone. A lone aircraft can fly much lower than a pair, and can get in and out of terrain much more easily, especially in marginal weather conditions of the sort we find over Europe so much of the time. The only times we would send out a pair of tactical reconnaissance aircraft to the same target would be if it was very heavily defended and a back-up might be necessary in case one was lost, or if the target was so large – say, a very large troop concentration – that it required more than one aircraft to photograph it.'

A great deal has been said about the value of information from reconnaissance satellites, and there can be no doubt that both before and during a conflict they would produce much useful intelligence. But it should be borne in mind that satellites, like every other military system, do have limitations. A satellite can do things that are impossible for a tactical reconnaissance aircraft, but there are also things a tactical reconnaissance aircraft can do that are impossible for a satellite:

'If photographs are required of a certain target, an RF-4C can be ordered to fly to the target to take them. It is not so for a satellite. Because of the physical problems of putting one into a particular orbit, once it is up there it cannot be re-positioned without an extraordinary amount of effort. And if the satellite is not looking towards the required target as it comes past, there is nothing you can do to make it. Moreover, a satellite observing part of Central Europe will do so only once per orbit, that is about once every eighty minutes. Because of the rotation of the Earth, the satellite flies over a different part of the Earth on each orbit; if it misses the target on one orbit – for example, because of cloud cover, an ever-present problem in Europe – it might not see it again for three days. That is why low-flying tactical reconnaissance aircraft are so valuable: we can go and look at targets at times when cloud prevents other systems from observing the ground.'

Carrying the most modern systems of any reconnaissance type operated by 2 ATAF, the 1st Tactical Reconnaissance Squadron provides a range of capabilities which makes it a particularly important part of the force:

'A key element for this particular unit is our value to the army commander at night. He has very few 'eyes' at night. Because of our AAD-5 and Pave Tack infra-red systems, and our navigation and radar capability, we can fly sorties and provide information to a commander by day or night. We are one of the very few reconnaissance units in 2 ATAF able to do that. In a conflict I think we would be assigned mainly to night operations, leaving other units to do the daylight reconnaissance. On the other hand, there would be far more requests for reconnaissance information by day because that is when most of the battles would be fought and the information needed quickly. So I think that while we would not fly exclusively at night, that would be when our unique capabilities would be of greatest value to the commander.'

The use of radio data-link to broadcast, in flight, the information gathered by TEREC is a pointer to the way ahead for future aerial reconnaissance systems. The Pave Tack video picture cannot be transmitted in this way, though it is well within the state of current technology to do so and any follow-on system will undoubtedly have this facility. The whole thrust of modern reconnaissance is to get the information to the users as rapidly as possible:

'The faster we can get the reconnaissance information to the guys who need it, the better. Reconnaissance has now reached the point where we are getting away from photography. If we can transmit data electronically in the form of a video picture, or give the battle commander the essential elements of information he wants, he doesn't need a photograph. In the case of an airfield attack, all the commander needs to know is if the runway has been cut and if repairs are going to take, say, twelve hours, and he is not going to need to send in another strike before then.

In years to come we will be able to data-link this information back to the control centre within one or two minutes of flying through the target area. And the battle commander will be able to see on his TV screen the pictures we have taken.'

Summing up, Carl Loveland stressed the vital importance of reconnaissance to support NATO air and land operations in any future conflict. It is the cornerstone of any effective response to an attack:

'I have been in reconnaissance, on and off, for fourteen years. It is a vitally important but usually unsung part of air operations. Much of the glamour goes to the people who shoot aircraft down or drop bombs and destroy things. But those who know 'the big picture' of what war is really about certainly understand the vital importance of reconnaissance; for unless a commander knows where the enemy forces are located and where they are concentrating, he will not be able to attack them to maximum effect.'

11: The Tank-Swatters

Lieutenant-Colonel Wilf Hyde-Smith joined the British Army in 1965 and was commissioned into the 15th/19th King's Royal Hussars, where he was a troop leader commanding four tanks. He trained as a helicopter pilot in 1968 and afterwards flew with units in Hong Kong and Brunei. In 1972 and 1973 he commanded a flight with No. 652 Squadron, which pioneered helicopter anti-tank operations in the British Army. In 1973 he became an instructor at the helicopter school at Middle Wallop in England and led the Army Air Corps helicopter display team, the 'Blue Eagles'. There followed a series of staff appointments, then, in 1981, with the rank of major, he took command of No. 653 Squadron operating Lynx and Gazelle helicopters in the anti-tank role at Soest in Germany. After completion of this tour at the end of 1984, he was promoted to his present rank and returned to Middle Wallop to serve on the staff of the Army Air Corps.

No. 653 Squadron is one of the anti-tank helicopter squadrons assigned to the 3rd Armoured Division, part of No. 1 British Corps in Germany, and has an establishment of eight Westland Lynx missile-carriers and four Westland Gazelles for reconnaissance. The Lynx is produced jointly in Britain and France and is a twin-engined, medium-weight, general-purpose helicopter; in the anti-tank role it carries a crew of two, a pilot and an air gunner who controls the missiles, and at take-off in the combat configuration it weighs just over 3 tons. Also built jointly by Britain and France, the Gazelle is a single-engined, lightweight general-purpose helicopter; in the reconnaissance role it carries a crew of two, a pilot and an observer, but no armament; at take-off in this configuration it weighs about 1½ tons. At low altitude the maximum speed of the Gazelle is about 150 knots; that of the Lynx is slightly lower. As currently equipped, No. 653

Squadron is able to carry out anti-tank operations only by day.

A dictionary defines the verb 'swat' as: 'hit with a short, crushing blow'. It is an apt term to describe an anti-tank helicopter attack on an enemy armoured force. When operating in the anti-tank role the Lynx carries eight TOW missiles. TOW (Tube-launched, Optically tracked, Wire-guided) is a well-proven missile which has been in service for more than a decade and has seen action in Vietnam and in the Middle East. It weighs 46 lb at launch, of which 8.6 lb is a shaped-charge warhead able to pierce the frontal armour of most tanks and the side armour of all of them. The missile has a maximum range of 3,750 metres, but its most effective range is between 1,500 and 2,500 metres.

Compared with fixed-wing jet combat aircraft, the helicopter is a slow machine with a short range, vulnerable to fire from even the smallest infantry weapons. Because of this, anti-tank helicopters would not normally fly over areas held by enemy forces. The principal role of the anti-tank helicopter is to halt enemy armoured thrusts which have broken through the main defensive line, thereby gaining time for ground forces to move into place to stabilize the position. Until required, the anti-tank helicopter units would normally be held in reserve at their camouflaged bases beyond the range of enemy artillery, some twenty to thirty miles from the battle area.

To survive in the battle area, helicopter pilots use what they call 'nap-of-the-earth' flying, making maximum use of contours and ground cover to limit their exposure to enemy fire. Wilf Hyde-Smith described this type of flying:

'When flying nap-of-the-earth one feels more an infantryman than an aviator. It is more akin to being in an airborne Land Rover than a low-level fast jet. It is important to avoid being silhouetted against the skyline, so wherever possible we fly along folds in the ground. One does not usually need to go particularly fast, nor, if there is good cover, does one need to go particularly low. If, for example, there was a significant valley on our side of the battle area, it would not be necessary to fly along the bottom of the valley; we need to go just low enough so the enemy cannot see us. Only when we had to

cross relatively exposed stretches of ground would we fly very
low and fast. And when I say 'very low' I mean cabbage-top-
height, slowing to walking pace to sneak under electricity or
telephone wires, using all the stealth we possibly could. If we
had to cross areas where there was no cover, we would fly as
fast as the helicopter would go, to reach the next bit of cover as
quickly as possible to reduce to an absolute minimum the time
we would be a potential target. Finally, approaching the firing
position, we would edge forward in a slow hover, moving little
faster than walking pace.'

A typical helicopter anti-tank operation might begin when the
ground force commander realized that his troops could not
contain an enemy armoured thrust. He would then give orders
for one or more of his squadrons to prepare to go into action. On
receiving this order a helicopter squadron commander would
dispatch a pair of Gazelles to begin watching the threatened
area.

'The Gazelles would fly to a position from which they could
see the enemy column. Their pilots would make full use of
nap-of-the-earth flying to keep out of sight, keeping close to
the ground and avoiding being 'skylined', going around hills
and clumps of trees, using valleys, fire-breaks in woods. Once
a helicopter crew had sighted the enemy they would pull back
into cover, make their report and then move to the next
sighting position. The task of the Gazelles would be to keep
the brigade or division commander, and the helicopter squadron commander, fully informed on the progress of the enemy
column.'

The Gazelles conducting such a reconnaissance would take it in
turn to move forward into sighting positions, with the rear
machine remaining a safe distance behind, watching for any
enemy reaction; if the leading helicopter stumbled upon an
enemy position and was shot down, it would be important that
this hard-won information was reported to headquarters. The
army headquarters would collate information from all sources,
including ground reconnaissance troops, to build up a detailed

picture of the composition, speed and direction of advance of the enemy force.

The reconnaissance phase of the operation would last until the enemy force reached a point from which it could be attacked, and this could take several hours:

'The Gazelle has an endurance of 2½ hours, so it can stay on station a long time keeping an eye on enemy movements. If the first pair of helicopters began to run short of fuel, they would be replaced by another pair, so there would always be at least two Gazelles watching the enemy advance.'

Some days or weeks previously, immediately after arriving in its new area, each helicopter squadron would have made a thorough reconnaissance of the area in which it might have to go into action. A divisional area of responsibility might have a frontage of 10 to 20 miles and a depth of 30 to 40 miles. In aviation terms that is a very small area, so pilots could become intimately familiar with its terrain and landmarks and they would have registered every firing position in the area from which they could engage enemy tanks if there was a break-through. An ideal site from which to mount a helicopter ambush would be an undulating tree-covered hillside, running parallel to and overlooking a wide area of farm land across which the enemy armoured force was about to pass. The Lynxes would be able to move into their firing positions unseen along one of the undula-tions, or perhaps a fire-break. Then they would spread out in line abreast well spaced out, and launch their missiles at the enemy armoured vehicles over the trees with the wooded hill behind to prevent them being silhouetted against the skyline. For an optimum engagement the target vehicles should be between 1,500 and 2,500 metres in front of the helicopter firing positions, and moving across the line of fire so that the missiles would strike the sides of the tanks where their armour was not as thick as the front. A poor area for anti-tank helicopter operations would be one where there was very little or no cover; or where there was too much cover to allow the helicopter crews to get clear shots with their long-range missiles.

Helicopters operating in the anti-tank role have a major

advantage over fixed-wing types in that they are able to select
the place, the time and the circumstances under which they
engage an enemy armoured force, to a degree that is impossible
for conventional attack aircraft. And if the advancing enemy
column is not in a position suitable for them to launch their
attack, the helicopters can afford to wait until they are. The
rolling countryside around the inner German border, punctu-
ated with numerous wooded areas of all sizes, is almost tailor-
made for anti-tank helicopter operations. There is scarcely an
area where an armoured force could move 10 miles without
passing one or more points from which it could be engaged in
this way.

During the reconnaissance phase of the operation the squadron's missile-carrying Lynx helicopters would be sitting on the
ground at their forward base, with crews strapped in and ready
to move immediately they received the order. From the helicopters' forward base, no enemy incursion into the divisional area
would be more than fifteen to twenty minutes flying time away,
and often it would be a good deal less. Armed with a continual
flow of detailed information on the position and rate of advance
of the enemy force, the commander of the helicopter squadron
would wait until his prey was about twenty minutes away from a
previously selected 'killing zone'. Then he would order the
Lynxes to take off and move into position for the ambush:

'The firing positions in the area would all have been recon-
noitred previously and the helicopter crews would have them
marked on their maps. The commander would select a
suitable one ahead of the enemy advance, and all he need say
would be the designation of the fire position and the time, for
example: 'Fire position Zulu 311, be there at 1535 hours.'

The commander would try to time things so that the Lynxes
could move straight into the firing positions with as little
hanging about as possible. The ideal would be that the Lynxes
arrived at their firing positions just as the enemy force reached
the 'killing zone' in front of them. Then the helicopters could
begin their attack immediately. But in a real war that is not
going to happen very often. After the Lynxes had taken off, the
enemy armoured force might pause near cover to refuel or

re-group, and so not reach the area in front of the designated firing position at the time expected.'

It is important for the Lynxes not to arrive at the firing points too early, otherwise they would have to wait about in the hover risking discovery by the enemy. So if the helicopter commander saw that the enemy forces had been delayed, he would order the Lynxes to a pre-planned waiting point:

'Our helicopters would go to a waiting point some miles away from the 'killing zone', typically somewhere in dead ground along the side of a wood just back from the battle area, where they would sit on the ground with engines idling and await developments. When the enemy advance resumed, the Lynxes would lift off and move to the ambush position.'

The officer leading the helicopter attack would normally control his force from a Gazelle, from which he would keep the enemy force under observation. As the column neared the designated 'killing zone' he would pass final instructions to the Lynxes to move towards their firing positions. From now on the operation would have about it the air of low cunning one would expect from a well-organized gang of street muggers and their look-outs, setting a trap for unsuspecting victims.

The minimum force for an engagement of this type would be one squadron; the maximum – if the enemy break-through was large enough to justify it and there were firing points giving sufficient cover – might be as many as three squadrons with up to twenty-four Lynxes. As well as directing his own attack, the helicopter leader would co-ordinate it with those of other friendly forces in the area:

'The important thing to remember is that the attack would be integrated with operations by other army units in the area; it would not be solely an air action. From his Gazelle the commander would be talking on the radio on the brigade or divisional artillery control net. He would give a time when his attack would begin and might ask the artillery to put down a barrage on the enemy force just before, to force the tank crews to 'close down'. With only their periscopes to see what was going on outside, that would limit their field of view considerably and reduce their chances of seeing our helicopters.'

During the artillery barrage the Lynxes would edge into their firing positions. As they did so, the helicopter squadron commander would assign crews to individual targets, with the aim of knocking out the key vehicles in the enemy column with the initial missile salvo: mine-clearing tanks leading the advance, the enemy force commander's tank if this could be identified, and anti-aircraft gun or missile systems which might be used against the helicopters. Once these had been dealt with, the helicopters would concentrate on picking off individual tanks.

Viewing the vehicles through powerful ×12 magnification binocular sites, the missile operators, termed 'airgunners', would have little difficulty in distinguishing their targets. At the designated time the artillery fire would cease, and as the dust began to clear the helicopter commander would order his force to launch their missiles *simultaneously*. The rocket motor in the rear of each TOW fires for one second to accelerate it to over 600 m.p.h. then the salvo of deadly missiles would coast the rest of the way to the target. The brief flashes from the rear of each rocket would scarcely be visible to those in the target area, even if they happened to be looking in the right direction:

'Each helicopter carries eight TOW missiles, but an airgunner can control only one at a time. Looking through the binocular sight, the gunner moves his joystick controller to keep an illuminated cross over the target vehicle. The act of doing this steers the missile along the line of sight until it impacts the target. After his first missile impacts, the operator re-aligns his sight on the next target and launches his second missile. TOW is extremely accurate and we would aim to use one missile against each target.

If everything had gone according to plan, the first the enemy knew of the attack would be when up to twenty-four tanks and other key vehicles in his force suddenly burst into flames; then, between ten and twenty seconds later, depending on the helicopters' firing range, a whole lot more would go

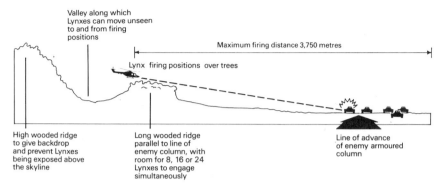

Valley along which
Lynxes can move unseen
to and from firing
positions

Maximum firing distance 3,750 metres

Lynx firing positions over trees

High wooded ridge
to give backdrop
and prevent Lynxes
being exposed above
the skyline

Long wooded ridge
parallel to line of
enemy column, with
room for 8, 16 or 24
Lynxes to engage
simultaneously

Line of advance
of enemy armoured
column

Attack on enemy armoured force by anti-tank helicopters

up; and within another 20 seconds, more still. That would certainly make a tank battalion commander's eyes water – if that is not shock action, I don't know what is! Without doubt it would throw an enemy column into complete and utter chaos and bring their advance to a halt until they could sort themselves out.'

The success of the ambush would hinge on the helicopter force remaining undetected until the first volley of missiles began to burst around the target vehicles. As this author has seen for himself, the chances of their achieving surprise are very high indeed. The Army Air Corps has a demonstration it is fond of laying on when it wants to make this point. Those to be indoctrinated are placed on open ground and told that they are under observation from a Lynx in a TOW firing position, in a certain clump of trees about 2,000 metres away. None of those in the party with the author was able to see the green-painted Lynx with the naked eye. On a radio order the helicopter rose above cover and switched on its landing lights to reveal its position. Then the landing lights were switched off and the Lynx sank back until only its rotor disc was above cover. Even when one knew exactly where to look and used binoculars, it was still difficult to pick out the helicopter; and this observer had far fewer distractions than there would have been for the crewman of a tank on the move.

After the initial missile salvoes had revealed the presence of the helicopters, the enemy could be expected to react violently:

'We would never launch more than four missiles from one firing position, because by the end of that time the position would have been compromised. Once they realized what was happening they would probably get their artillery to put down a barrage on our firing positions. We would not want to be around when that happened as we are vulnerable to any sort of fire: from anti-aircraft guns, artillery, tanks or infantry. Even a rifle bullet hitting a helicopter in the right place could bring it down.

If there were still targets in the area and other suitable firing positions from which to engage them, we might move around and repeat the whole thing from a different direction. Or the Lynxes might go back to a replenishment point, to refuel and take on more missiles ready for the next action.'

After such a mauling the enemy column might be halted for an hour or more, its vehicles sitting in an untidy mass while officers struggled to re-group the force before it could resume the advance. During this period it would make an ideal target for attack aircraft, which could cause further delays and allow the army more time to move blocking units into place ahead of the enemy force to seal off the incursion.

A possible way for the enemy to counter such an attack would be to send armed helicopters to nose around potential firing positions on the flanks of the advancing column, to flush out the Lynxes. Such an enterprise could prove hazardous for the enemy helicopters, however. To do the job properly they would have to fly low and slow around the periphery of a large number of wooded areas, some of which would contain hostile infantry. Even armoured helicopters are vulnerable to fire at short range from infantry weapons and shoulder-launched anti-aircraft missiles. Moreover, the Lynxes themselves would not be without right of reply: although it was not designed as an air-to-air missile, TOW could be effective against slow-flying helicopters and would make a nasty mess of any it hit. Nor would enemy fighters find it any more rewarding to mount search-and-destroy missions against the helicopters flying nap-of-the-earth over their own territory, under the protection of battlefield air defence weapons.

We have seen how one experienced commander believes the anti-tank helicopter might be used in a future conflict in Europe. Certainly its theoretical capability is impressive but, like so many modern weapons, it has never been proved in war:

'It is true that the anti-tank helicopter has never really been proved in war. We are looking at the Iran–Iraq war with interest; a few anti-tank helicopters have been used there but not in any great numbers. But we have tried out the tactics extensively on manoeuvres and we are confident that our operating procedures will work.

I believe the anti-tank helicopter to be an extremely useful weapon system in any future conflict. What other weapon system can move at 120 knots over a distance of up to 50 miles, at short notice and unhindered by difficult terrain, to take on an unexpected enemy armoured thrust; and when it gets there launch a snap attack to pick off selectively twenty or forty or sixty of the most important vehicles within a space of two minutes? And five minutes later those same helicopters could be doing the same thing to another enemy armoured force, or to the previous one from a different direction. What other system can do all that?'

The question is rhetorical: no other weapon system can do that. Proven or not, the 'tank-swatting' helicopter poses a formidable potential threat to armoured forces attempting Blitzkrieg-type advances in any future conflict.

12: The Electronic Foxers

Lieutenant-Colonel David Vesely joined the US Air Force in 1965, and after pilot training became a flying instructor. In 1971 and 1972 he flew UH-1N helicopter gunships in Vietnam in support of special operations. On his return to the USA he served the next three years as an engineering officer with a Minuteman intercontinental ballistic missile wing at Grand Forks, North Dakota. In 1975 he resumed his flying career and joined the 366th Tactical Fighter Wing flying F-111Fs at Mountain Home, Idaho. He was with the wing in 1977 when it moved to Lakenheath in England. In 1979 he went to Staff College, and was afterwards posted to the NATO Southern Region air headquarters at Naples, Italy. In 1982 he was posted to Upper Heyford in England, responsible for managing the introduction of the EF-111 aircraft into the European theatre; and when the 42nd Electronic Combat Squadron was activated with this aircraft in July 1983, he became its commander.

The 42nd Electronic Combat Squadron is based at Upper Heyford in England and is established at thirteen General Dynamics EF-111 Raven radar-jamming aircraft. These aircraft are modified from F-111 attack aircraft with characteristics that are similar to the F-111E described in Chapter 4. The EF-111 carries a crew of two, a pilot and an electronic warfare officer (EWO) who navigates the aircraft and operates the radar jamming equipment.

Since 1944 several types of combat aircraft have been modified for the radar-jamming role, to carry electronic countermeasures equipment in place of bombs to enable them to support attacks by other aircraft. At the time of writing the most important aircraft of this type available to support NATO air operations in Europe is the EF-111. These aircraft are all converted F-111As, many of them the early production models of the aircraft dating back to 1967. But although parts of them are old, the aircraft have been reworked to such an extent that they are virtually new machines:

'It is a massive conversion, which takes almost a year. The aircraft is completely stripped down, the wings are removed, all of the electrical wiring is pulled out and the aircraft is completely rewired. The major changes include a re-designed cockpit with much of the equipment repositioned. The weapons bay in the fuselage is restructured to house the ALQ-99 tactical jamming system with ten jamming transmitters covering several frequency bands. The ball on the top of the fin houses the directional receivers which control the jammers. For its self-protection the aircraft also carries an ALQ-137 internal electronic countermeasure system, chaff and infra-red decoy dispensers, and radar warning receivers.

To provide the necessary additional power for the jammers, the EF-111 is fitted with larger alternators than the A model. And to carry away excess heat from the jammers the EF-111 is fitted with an extensive cooling system.'

The self-protection electronic countermeasures systems carried by attack aircraft are intended to jam only the radars used to aim guns or missiles at that aircraft, and only for as long as they are trying to engage it. Such jammers are relatively small, low-powered and designed to jam only for short periods; moreover, their aerials are designed to radiate in all directions to give all-round cover. The ALQ-99 tactical jamming system fitted to the EF-111 is somewhat different. It was designed to jam several enemy long-range radars simultaneously, from orbit lines over friendly territory, and to do so for long periods. To achieve this the ALQ-99 employs ten separate high-powered jamming transmitters, each feeding a directional aerial located in the streamlined radome under the fuselage. The complex receiver system of the ALQ-99, with aerials in the streamlined blister on top of the fin, sorts out the plethora of incoming radar signals and from these establishes the frequencies and relative bearings of radars in the area. The EWO selects those he requires to jam, jamming transmitters are tuned to their frequencies and their associated directional aerials are trained on the victim radars. By focusing jamming at selected enemy radars in this way, in both frequency and direction, the ALQ-99 makes the most effective use of the available radiated power.

David Vesely went on to describe the ways in which the EF-111 would be used to support attack aircraft:

'There are three basic roles of the EF-111. The first is what we call 'stand-off jamming', orbiting quite high up and jamming from well over friendly territory beyond the reach of the enemy air defences. Using these tactics we would jam the enemy long-range early-warning radars to screen the movement of friendly aircraft in our area.

The second role is 'close-in jamming', where we would be much closer to the enemy radars but still over friendly territory. The jamming power we put into the enemy radars increases the nearer we are to them, so we would use this tactic if we needed to hit their sets with a lot of power. In this case we would be close to the friendly aircraft we were screening, though not in formation with them. We would fly as low as possible, just high enough to beam our jamming into the enemy radars.

The third role is 'jamming escort', providing jamming protection for forces making deep penetration attacks on heavily defended targets. It was for this role that the F-111 was chosen over other types for conversion for the electronic combat aircraft role: it is the only aircraft in the US Air Force inventory with the performance and the range to accompany any other NATO tactical aircraft to and from its target.'

Although a single EF-111 can provide a useful amount of jamming, except on some of the jamming escort missions these aircraft would usually operate in co-ordinated pairs:

'In each of these roles the F-111 can operate as a single aircraft. However, we prefer to send aircraft out in pairs in case one goes unserviceable, in which case there is another to go in and do the job. Also, with two planes there is twice as much jamming power being radiated as with one.

It is unlikely that we would use more than two EF-111s in the same immediate area. For one thing, we have insufficient aircraft; and for another we tend to work in what we call 'airspace bubbles', and if there are more than two of our airraft in the same bubble, things can then get very complicated.'

Just about the only thing to be said against the EF-111 is that there are far too few of them. Only forty-two F-111s are to be modified into electronic combat aircraft, and in a major conflict there would probably be far more uses for EF-111s than there were aircraft. Certainly Vesely's unit would be hard pushed to support more than a small proportion of the air operations taking place in Europe:

'I know Air Marshal Hine and the other commanders would love to have enough EF-111s to send one or two to escort each of their package formations going deep into enemy territory. But unfortunately we do not have enough EF-111s to do that. There is another EF-111 squadron in the USA, and in a war it could come here, though not if there were more pressing commitments in the Pacific or somewhere else.

How best should we use the few EF-111s we have? I think we would be unwise to spread our small number of electronic combat aircraft evenly across the battle area and hope to achieve anything worthwhile. The EF-111s would be spread too wide and too thin, and would probably disrupt very little of the enemy system. And they could not do it around the clock. Even if we used all forty-two EF-111s over Europe there would not be enough to cause continual disruption of the enemy defences.'

An important part of David Vesely's job is to give presentations on the role of his squadron at headquarters and combat units throughout Europe, trying to put over a balanced view of what the EF-111 can do:

'Indoctrination is an important part of my job. I am constantly giving briefings, trying to explain what the EF-111 is, what electronic combat is, and what they are not. It is important to explain what the airplane can do. But in a lot of cases the discussion centres on what it cannot do. At first there were many people who thought, 'Here is the EF-111, our shiny new electronic combat airplane, the panacea which is going to blind the enemy radars completely . . .' Well, that is not so, simply because of the large number of radars the other side has and the small number of EF-111s we have. We are not going to be able to blanket out all the enemy radars from Denmark to the Alps. That just isn't going to happen and we have said so.

When we visit other combat units they sometimes ask, 'How should we change our tactics to take best advantage of your being there to support us?' And my answer to them is, 'Don't change a thing. Assume we are not there.' The reason I say that is they can have no assurance that an EF-111 will be there to support them on a given mission. So if there is an EF-111 in position to support them, fine; if it isn't, they will be no worse off. But if they had altered their tactics to depend on us and for some reason we were not in the area, they could be in trouble. And even if there was an EF-111 in their area, there could be no guarantee that it was jamming the specific radar looking at them.'

In David Vesely's view, one very effective way to exploit the EF-111's unique capabilities would be to use it in concert with other electronic combat systems to neutralize the enemy air defence system in a limited area for a limited time. Here he repeats the familiar arguments on the need to concentrate forces in space and time, though in the context of electronic combat operations:

'One way would be to use our electronic combat systems in complementary packages. The EF-111 is not the only electronic combat system; there are the F-4 'Wild Weasels' to attack the surface-to-air missile batteries, the EC-130H Compass Call aircraft to jam the enemy communications, the Army's ground jammers. These work in different ways to counter different parts of the enemy defences. By combining the capabilities of our electronic combat systems, we can cover the bulk of the enemy radars and communications in a specified area, and so deny him the ability to track our aircraft for a limited time. The aim is to force the enemy into the worst situation we can, then run our attack aircraft through while the defences are too confused to stop them.

Virtually all NATO aircraft which are going to make deep penetrations into enemy territory carry some sort of ECM self-protection system. But that is only to counter 'the shooters', the radars used to aim the anti-aircraft guns or missiles. If the attack force is seen a long way out and the defenders have time to prepare to meet our aircraft before they come within firing range, in spite of their self-protection systems some of our aircraft are liable to be hit. So one of the jobs of the EF-111s is to cut the warning time available to the enemy to a minimum.

That is the concept we are trying to get across: concentrate the electronic combat force, give it a specific mission or objective for a fairly short period of time – say, an hour or two. We think that would be much better than spreading the EF-111s along the whole battle front to try to cause continual disruption, which they could not do effectively.'

For much of the time low-flying attack aircraft would be out of the view of enemy ground radars anyway, and any jamming support they received from the EF-111s would come as a bonus. But it is possible that in the future EF-111s might be called upon to play a considerably more dominant part in a land–air battle. Used imaginatively, they could bring about a fundamental change in the way deep penetration attacks are mounted:

'The tactics used by our attack forces are continually being re-examined in the light of experience gained during exercises flown in Europe and in the USA. Recently General Donnelly, the Commander in Chief Allied Air Forces in Central Europe, has forced us to re-think how we would fight an air war. For many years we have thought the best way for aircraft to penetrate to targets deep in enemy territory is to go in fast and at very low altitude. He is concerned that in some circum-

stances this could be more dangerous than if we routed our
attack aircraft in at higher altitudes, protected by aircraft like
the EF-111.

   What he is saying is, basically, 'Why are we going in low
and fast, perhaps through miserable weather, with pilots
risking running into the ground and killing themselves without the enemy having to do anything? Why don't we go in at
higher altitude?' Everyone answers, 'Because of the defences
. . .' And he is saying, 'Well, wait a minute, let's take another
look at those defences.' While we have been going lower and
lower and faster and faster, the enemy has built up an efficient
defence system to counter low-flying, fast-moving targets.
Now if we take a close look at those parts of the defences able
to engage our aircraft flying at higher altitudes, perhaps we
can find some areas where they are less dense than those lower
down. And if the EF-111s and 'Wild Weasels' can jam out or
neutralize some of those systems, maybe that could be a less
dangerous place to route in some of our attack formations. He
is not saying that is necessarily what we are going to do, he is
saying that we should not suffer from tunnel-vision with our
tactics, and the low-altitude approach may not necessarily be
the best under all circumstances.'

Combat aircraft have always been able to tailor their tactics to
give the best chance of success on any particular mission. The
fact that a force penetrates all or part of the way to the target at
high altitude on one day does not preclude it from going in at
medium or low altitude on the following day. But the need to be
able to engage raiding forces coming in at high, medium or low
altitudes would greatly complicate the task of an air defence
system and force it to divide its strength to meet the separate
threats. Surface-to-air missile systems effective against high-
flying aircraft are usually ineffective against low-flyers, and vice
versa. David Vesely is following the debate with interest but has
yet to make up his own mind:

'My jury is still out. I was brought up in the 'go low go fast'
way of thinking and to my mind there are still a lot of plusses
for that. Radar pulses, missiles and bullets cannot go through

rocks. So if you can place a rock between you and the enemy weapons system, you know you are relatively safe. But it is very difficult to train to fly at low altitude at high speed without risking hitting the ground. So I think there is a lot to be said for flying higher. I am anxious to hear the discussions that result, now that General Donnelly has stirred the pot.

We must not stereotype our tactics, because if we do we will give away the key to air power and that is flexibility, keeping the enemy guessing on how we are going to do things.'

The EF-111 is extremely expensive, with a price tag of about $45 million each if one includes the original F-111. That is more than twice the cost of an attack aircraft like Tornado, and a lot to spend on an aircraft lacking any armament. But if there was a major conflict David Vesely is convinced that these specialized aircraft would recoup their cost many times over:

'The EF-111 is not going to cause any physical damage to the enemy, but that is not their purpose. Their task is to degrade the enemy's longer-range radars, to deprive him of warning of the approach of our attack forces and so allow less time to prepare his defence. By doing that they will enable more of our attack aircraft to return safely after their missions, and so be available to fly further sorties. That sums up the role of the EF-111: it is a 'losses reducer'.'

In April 1986, as this book was going to press, the 42nd Electronic Combat Squadron went into action for the first time. Three of its EF-111s flew from Upper Heyford to provide jamming support during the attack by F-111 bombers against targets in Libya.

13: The 'Wild Weasels'

Lieutenant-Colonel Les Kersey joined the US Air Force in 1965. After completing his pilot training he flew F-4 Phantoms in nuclear strike and ground attack roles with the 81st Tactical Fighter Squadron at Hahn, Germany. In 1970 he was posted to the 388th Tactical Fighter Wing at Korat in Thailand and logged more than 500 combat flying hours in Phantoms during the Vietnam War. On his return to the USA in 1971 he became a flying instructor at Columbus AFB Mississippi, then returned to South East Asia in 1975 as a weapons and tactics officer on the staff of Headquarters 7th Air Force in Thailand. Next came another tour on Phantoms with the 388th Tactical Fighter Wing, then based at Hill AFB, Utah. In 1978 he attended the US Army Command and General Staff College, and the following year served at the Pentagon in Washington in the office concerned with air defence suppression; while in that post he was planning officer directly responsible for the F-4G and also suppression of enemy air defences branch chief. Since 1983 he has been with the 52nd Tactical Fighter Wing based at Spangdahlem in Germany, the sole air defence suppression unit assigned to NATO; at the time of the interview he was assistant director of operations for the wing.

The 52nd Tactical Fighter Wing comprises the 23rd, the 81st and the 480th Tactical Fighter Squadrons, each with an establishment of eight F-4G Phantoms and sixteen F-4E Phantoms. The primary role of the wing is 'Wild Weasel' operations – the suppression or destruction of enemy ground radars and anti-aircraft missile systems. The F-4s operated by the 52nd TFW have performance characteristics similar to those of the RF-4Cs described in Chapter 10.

The F-4G version of the Phantom has been purpose-modified for the air defence suppression role:

'The F-4G is a highly modified version of the F-4E. The gun has been removed from the nose and in its place is a fairing which contains the extensive avionics suite necessary for the new role. The cockpit for the rear crewman, the electronic warfare officer, has been completely rebuilt.'

To enable the crew to find enemy anti-aircraft gun and missile batteries, the F-4G carries an APR-38 receiver which locates radars in the area by taking a series of bearings on their signals. This receiver is similar in its method of operation to the TEREC equipment fitted to RF-4C reconnaissance aircraft (see Chapter 10), but APR-38 is an attack system and the information it provides is more accurate and more immediately usable.

'Our job is to spend extended periods in areas where there are enemy surface-to-air missiles, so we need a sophisticated capability to be able to do that and survive. The problem of killing SAMs in enemy territory is a rather esoteric business. Less than one per cent of the vehicles in a Soviet motor-rifle division are to do with SAMs, and 'Wild Weasel' crews would not want to have to search through the other 99 per cent to find what they were after. So we have to sort the battlefield electronically to find that 1 per cent.

The APR-38 measures the bearings of signals from radars in the area, and feeds these into a computer which identifies their types and plots their positions on the scope in the EWO's position. Once the position of the enemy radar has been determined, this information is held in the memory of the computer and can be recalled even if the radar switches off.'

A typical war load for a 'Wild Weasel' F-4G is two Shrike radiation-homing missiles or four CBU-52 cluster bombs under the inboard wing pylons, and two Sparrow air-to-air missiles for self-protection and a fuel tank under the centre fuselage. At the time of writing, the Shrike is the main offensive weapon carried by 'Wild Weasel' aircraft:

'At present the only anti-radiation missile we carry is the AGM-45 Shrike, a first-generation missile which uses twenty-year-old technology. At low altitude it has a range of about five miles, and it carries a 150 lb warhead.

The CBU-52 is about the size of a 750 lb bomb, and is fitted with a radar fuse to release its sub-munitions at a pre-set height above the ground. It releases several hundred bomblets each about the size and shape of a softball and weighing about a pound. These bomblets explode on impact and are effective against soft-skinned vehicles and personnel. For our role the CBU-52 is a useful weapon: the vehicles belonging to a missile battery are not heavily armoured, and the radar antennas and the missiles on their launchers are considered 'soft' targets.'

The F-4E Phantoms operated by the 52nd Tactical Fighter Wing are standard fighter-bomber versions of the aircraft which, at the time of writing, carry no internal equipment specifically for the 'Wild Weasel' role:

'The F-4Es do not have the avionics to locate enemy radars precisely; they are dependent on the F-4Gs to tell them where the targets are. Normally the E models carry the same missile or bomb load as the G model they are working with.'

The F-4E still carries a 20 mm cannon under its nose, a relic of its previous fighter-bomber role. Les Kersey sees little use for this weapon for 'Wild Weasel' operations, however:

'I would liken attacking an enemy missile site with the gun to the Charge of the Light Brigade – very heroic, but not really a smart thing to do!'

In the 52nd Tactical Fighter Wing the F-4Gs and the F-4Es operate together in tactical pairs:

'Our standard employment element comprises two airplanes, an F-4G and an F-4E working as a mutually supporting pair. We might send four aircraft into a target area, but when they got there they would operate in autonomous pairs. For example, one pair might attack the radar at a missile site with anti-radiation missiles from one direction, as the second pair approached from a different direction to attack the missile launchers with cluster bombs.

Our more experienced crews fly the F-4Gs; they lead the aircraft elements. If I had the choice we would have seventy-two F-4Gs in the wing, but the F-4G is a very expensive aircraft and the Air Force doesn't have seventy-two to send over here. So we use the E model as an ordnance carrier to support the G model, to help deliver sufficient ordnance to the battle area.'

The fact that the 52nd TFW has twice as many F-4Es as F-4Gs stems from a recent reorganization which redistributed the wing's two squadrons of E-model aircraft and one squadron of G-models to form three mixed squadrons. At the time of writing further changes are planned which will result in Phantoms of both models in the unit receiving new avionic equipment to make them more effective in the role. The wing is also to receive the new HARM (High Speed Anti-Radiation) missile, a considerably more capable and longer-ranging weapon than the ageing Shrike. The new weapon is extremely expensive, however: informed sources put the cost of HARM at $400,000 each – uncomfortably close to the cost of some of the enemy systems it would be used against in time of war.

Les Kersey discussed the philosophy behind air defence suppression operations, and described how widely differing systems would be brought together to achieve success in this role:

'Defence suppression is divided into two areas, what we call 'hard kill' and 'soft kill'. A hard kill is the destruction of an enemy system using missiles or bombs. A soft kill is the use of electronic countermeasures to confuse a system for a given time.

When we talk about defence suppression we are talking about a combination of hard-kill and soft-kill techniques. When 'Wild Weasels' went into the battle area they would usually have support from EF-111s giving stand-off jamming or close-in jamming. We might also have EC-130 'Compass

Call' Hercules aircraft jamming enemy air defence radio communications in the area.

To attack an enemy radar site accurately I would need it to keep transmitting, particularly while my Shrike anti-radiation missiles were in flight. If the radar were to shut down they would have nothing to home on. That is where EC-130 'Compass Call' and EF-111 aircraft could help us.

In an integrated air defence system there would be long-range EW/GCI [Early Warning/Ground Controlled Interception] radars keeping watch on the skies above the area and feeding data on the positions of target aircraft to the SAM batteries. If a SAM battery was 'netted' into the main air defence system in this way it would be extremely difficult for a 'Wild Weasel' team to attack it. The radar operators at the enemy missile battery would know where our aircraft were and when they were in range; they could switch on their fire-control radar for short periods, engage one of our aircraft, then switch off again. The missile control radar – the one we would be after – would be on for too short a time for us to attack it.

But if EF-111s were jamming the EW/GCI radars in that area, and a 'Compass Call' EC-130 jammed the air defence radio communications network, that SAM battery would have to use its own short-range radars to locate targets before it could engage them. The fire-control radar would have to transmit for much longer and that would give the 'Wild Weasel' team a much better chance to attack it with Shrike.'

Les Kersey outlined the method of operation of a 'Wild Weasel' F-4s team within this scenario:

'The pair of 'Weasel' aircraft would approach the target area at low altitude in regular fighter defensive formation, extended line abreast. When it reached the target area the F-4G would pop up to about 600 feet just outside the range of the enemy SAM batteries, to enable its APR-38 to get a quick series of bearings on the enemy systems. The aircraft would then return to low altitude, move to another position and repeat the procedure.

It takes a few minutes for the APR-38 to arrive at a solution. It needs at least three bearings on a radar from separate points to establish its location; accuracy depends on the width of the angle at which the bearings cut each other, the more cuts the better. If the F-4G could stay above the radar horizon in the target area for a full minute, the APR-38 could plot all the radars in the area. But I would not particularly want to spend sixty seconds in a defended area exposed in that way. So the F-4G would 'work' the signals with a series of pop-ups from low altitude, to build what I call a 'situation awareness' of the electronic battlefield around it.'

When the APR-38 has 'cased' the area, the EWO in the rear cockpit of the F-4G would see on his TV-type screen a plan view of the area centred on the aircraft's position, with different symbols to indicate the positions and types of those radars that had been radiating:

'The EWO can identify the radars out there, the EW/GCI sets, the missile and gun fire control radars. Crews would be briefed on an order of priority of systems to attack. EW/GCI radars would be very high priority targets if we went deep enough into hostile territory to be in their area. The order of priority of the air defence systems would usually start with the medium-range missiles [for example, the SA-4 and the SA-6] and work down to the short-range systems [for example, the SA-8]. The ZSU 23-4 mobile anti-aircraft gun would be a low-priority target; there would probably be so many of them in the battle area that it would not be worth our while to attack them.

The preferred attack method would be initially with anti-radiation missiles, followed by a direct attack with cluster bombs.'

While the F-4G was plotting the locations of the enemy radars, its supporting F-4E would remain at low altitude in formation with it, providing cover, ready to ward off enemy fighters attempting to interfere with the operation or providing warning of enemy surface weapons trying to engage the pair. Once an air defence battery had been selected as target and its position refined, both Phantoms would run in to make a co-ordinated attack with Shrikes or cluster bombs:

'The mere presence of 'Weasels' in an area might scare enemy radar operators into becoming defensively minded and shutting down their sets. If they did, they would not be able to engage the aircraft we were supporting, and we would have done our job. If the enemy comes up with his radar, I'm going to kill him; if he shuts down, that is fine with me, my heart rate stays relatively low that day . . .'

Like a matador playing a bull, a 'Wild Weasel' team 'working' an enemy missile battery would have to do so with the very greatest care: the hunter could become the hunted with little or no warning. No 'Wild Weasel' crewman is allowed to forget that during the initial operations of this type over North Vietnam in 1965 the unit involved lost five of its seven aircraft in rapid succession. It is a difficult and demanding role which in war would present many dangers:

'The mission calls for crews to fly and navigate over hostile territory at high speed at low altitude, 500 feet and below, with periods of high-g manoeuvring during which the aircraft is within two seconds of hitting the ground at any given time. And in wartime they would have to do it while being shot at. The enemy would probably know if 'Weasel' aircraft were in the area, because the F-4Gs have to pop up to see where the radars are and that means the enemy could see them.

Flying the F-4G in the 'Wild Weasel' role often pushes crews into what we call 'task saturation', when the workload is so high that even experienced crews are pushed to the limit. The APR-38 and the computer sort out the radar signals, but the EWO still has to operate these systems and analyse and interpret what he sees on the screens.'

For self-protection the 'Wild Weasel' aircraft carry ALQ-131 electronic countermeasures pods, and chaff and infra-red flare dispensers. The computer-controlled ALQ-131 pod is particularly suitable for use in the 'Wild Weasel' role. It automatically selects the optimum mode of jamming to counter the radar of the enemy system trying to engage the aircraft.

Although 'Wild Weasel' aircraft might be used to escort night and all-weather attack aircraft, F-111s and Tornadoes, going after very high value targets, Les Kersey does not see this as the main role for his wing in time of war:

'In my opinion, an F-111 or a Tornado going against most targets at 540 knots at 200 feet at night wouldn't need a whole lot of help from us. The people who would really want our help would be the daylight attack aircraft like the Harriers, the Alphajets, the Mirages, the NF-5s and the F-16s. Many of those don't carry self-protection electronic countermeasures equipment. And none of them has terrain-following radar, which means that if the weather is marginal they will be unable to fly close to the ground and will be vulnerable to the defences. 'Wild Weasels' can greatly enhance the survivability of these types of attack aircraft.'

The sort of raid the 'Wild Weasels' would be most often called upon to support might be a force of perhaps forty attack aircraft on their way to a concentration of enemy tanks and other vehicles some 20 miles behind the battle area, perhaps bunched together and in some confusion after the destruction of a bridge they were to have crossed. However, if a large enemy armoured force had been brought to a halt, its air defence weapons would probably have been brought to a halt with it. To support such an attack operation as many as nine 'Wild Weasel' elements, eighteen aircraft, might be necessary:

'We can work that far beyond the battle area, but to do that we would first have to cross the battle area and the air defences there. I would liken that problem to asking an F-15 pilot to fly through one cloud of MiGs so he could get to a second cloud of MiGs beyond. I would question our ability to cross the battle area without having to engage some of the enemy SAM systems, and if 'Weasel' aircraft expend their ordnance there they will not have it to use against enemy systems in the target area.

In such a case we would use what we call a 'Rollback' technique against the enemy air defences in the battle area. We might send three pairs of 'Wild Weasel' aircraft into the area about five minutes before the main attack force was to go through, to 'work' those systems and plot the positions of the various enemy radars. Those 'Weasels' would then be ready to go into action immediately if the missile batteries they had plotted tried to engage the attack force as it came past. Flying with the main attack force might be six more elements of 'Weasels' with orders to attack enemy missile batteries only in the target area.'

There would never be any question of 'Wild Weasel' elements flying up and down the battle area looking for enemy air defence systems to attack. In Central Europe there would be simply too many enemy radars for such tactics to justify the risks:

'The 'Wild Weasel' mission is not an end in itself; we would be in an area to support other forces. If other aircraft were not in the area or about to enter the area, there would be no reason for 'Wild Weasel' aircraft to be there. Our sole task is to make it possible for the aircraft we support to complete their missions and survive in areas defended by the enemy.'

Having described the type of mission his wing might be called upon to undertake during a conflict in Central Europe, Les Kersey gave his own views on the likelihood of its ever having to do so:

'There has been a lot of thought and a lot of talk about the nature of a future war if there was one in Central Europe. In my personal view, if it happened there would be three or four or five days of extremely heavy fighting, with extremely heavy losses. Then both sides would be on the ropes, exhausted. The expenditure of missiles and bombs and bullets and the destruction of people and equipment would be so great that it would be impossible for either side to fight at that rate for very long.

After five or six days I think the level of violence would drop dramatically. The Russians would not want to fritter away the shield of forty or fifty divisions they have in Central Europe. And NATO would not want to fritter away its forces either. Both sides would know that if either started to run out of conventional forces the nuclear threshold would come down, and fast.

I think that if a war started in Central Europe it could happen only because of a miscalculation on one side or the other, it would not be a deliberate act. There would be no easy victory for either side. The cost in terms of lives and resources would be too phenomenal even to imagine. In my opinion a major war between NATO and Warsaw Pact forces in Central Europe is the least likely war to be fought. But if it happened, it would be the worst war ever to have to fight.'

14: Guardians of the Baltic Shore

Fregattenkapitaen (Commander) Volke Liche joined the German Navy in 1961. As is usual for officers entering that service, his training began with a three-year course as a seagoing officer which included a cruise in that Navy's sail training ship. After receiving his commission in 1964 he volunteered for the Naval Air Arm. Two years later, after pilot training, he joined No. 1 Staffel (squadron) of Marine Flieger Geschwader 2 with reconnaissance F-104s. He held a succession of flying posts within the Staffel and the Geschwader staff until 1975, when he took command of the Staffel. Between 1978 and 1980 he served at NATO headquarters in Brussels as an intelligence officer, then he returned to Marine Flieger Geschwader 2 as deputy commander of operations. In 1983 he converted to the Tornado and became commander of operations with Marine Flieger Geschwader 1, the first German unit to receive this aircraft.

Marine Flieger Geschwader 1 is based at Jagel in Schleswig-Holstein and has an established strength of forty-seven Tornado attack aircraft similar to those operated by the Royal Air Force and the German Air Force. The unit operates in conjunction with its sister unit, Marine Flieger Geschwader 2, equipped with F-104s and based nearby at Eggebek; MFG 2 is scheduled to re-equip with Tornadoes in the near future.

In any major conflict in Central Europe the two Marine Flieger Geschwader could not expect to be allowed to conduct their operations without enemy interference. Both Jagel and Eggebek are within seventy nautical miles – less than ten minutes' flying time – of the East German border; they are two of the furthest forward of the major NATO air bases. Airfields of such importance would be liable to frequent and heavy air attack, which would be bound to cause a measure of disruption even though their aircraft are housed in hardened shelters and vital facilities are protected by thick layers of concrete. Once airborne, the Tornadoes and F-104s could expect to be engaged by marauding enemy fighters at any time. If such a war began, it would test to the full the morale and combat capability of the aircrew and the groundcrew of the two units

The reason why the anti-shipping Tornadoes and F-104s are based so far east is that the Warsaw Pact maintains substantial amphibious forces in the Baltic area, together with the specialized landing ships and hovercraft to carry them into action. At the time of writing the Soviet Baltic Fleet operates more than 40 destroyers and escorts, and 250 smaller patrol craft, which would be used to cover such an operation. These forces pose a threat to the NATO states with shorelines on the Baltic: Germany and Denmark. The task of the two German Naval Air attack units is to ensure that any amphibious landing operation against NATO territory would be an extremely risky undertaking:

'Our job is to attack enemy surface shipping in the Baltic as far east as possible, and the success of such attacks would depend on our getting timely information on the movements of enemy naval forces. The Baltic is a very small area; to an ocean flyer it is like a bathtub. In a time of tension our Breguet Atlantic aircraft would fly continuous reconnaissance missions over the Baltic, but once the shooting started these slow aircraft would be unable to survive in that area and our Tornadoes and F-104s would have to take over the reconnaissance task. Our sister unit Marine Flieger Geschwader 2 has an F-104 reconnaissance Staffel capable of photographic and infra-red reconnaissance. And all the naval Tornadoes and F-104s can fly radar and visual reconnaissance missions.

Operating in the long-range reconnaissance role, Tornadoes would fly without offensive armament, carrying two drop tanks under the fuselage in additon to the two normally carried under the wings. With four tanks the Tornado has an endurance of about four hours, sufficient to take it along the Baltic as far east as Leningrad – more than 750 nautical miles from Jagel if the aircraft stays over the sea.

Our effort would be only one piece in the mosaic of NATO intelligence-gathering. NATO has many other means avail-

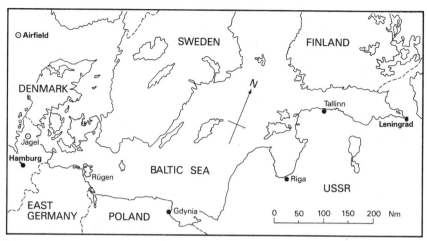

Marine Flieger Geschwader 1 operational area

able to it, including satellites, so we would expect to find out pretty early if the Soviets began moving naval infantry from their barracks to the ports and started to assemble amphibious landing ships.'

Tornadoes would fly such reconnaissance missions at low altitude, using their radar intermittently to scan the sea for ships in the area. For the rest of the time the aircraft would remain radar-silent to conceal their positions.

In its usual attack configuration a German Navy Tornado carries two Kormoran anti-ship missiles under the fuselage, two drop tanks and two ECM pods under the wings, and a self-defence armament of two Sidewinder missiles and two 27 mm cannon. The Kormoran is almost identical in concept and operation to the air-launched Exocet sea-skimming missile which first caught world attention during the Falklands conflict in 1982. The Kormoran weighs 1,300 lb and carries a 364 lb warhead; after launch a rocket motor accelerates the missile to just below sonic speed and it has a maximum range of about twenty nautical miles. Before launch the position of the target ship is fed into the missile, and after launch its self-contained navigation system guides it to that area. When the missile gets there its radar is switched on, it locks on the largest radar echo it can find and homes on it as it skims low over the sea. After it has been launched the Kormoran requires no further control from the launching aircraft; in modern parlance it is termed a 'fire-and-forget' weapon.

Kormoran is the main weapon employed by MFG 1, but its crews are also trained to attack ships with 1,000 lb, 500 lb and 250 lb bombs, ballistic and retarded, and BL755 cluster bombs.

Once hostilities had begun and an enemy naval force had been detected at sea and within its range, MFG 1 would expect orders to launch an attack:

'Let us consider an attack on the most difficult target from our point of view, a large convoy of landing ships carrying enemy amphibious troops. We could expect the landing ships to be in the centre of the force, with a screen of escorts around it and the screen strongest in the direction from which they expected us to attack. So if our main target is – as it must always be – the ships carrying the amphibious forces, we might have to knock out some of the escorts to get close enough to hit our main targets.

A convoy has to move at the speed of the slowest ship, and one with landing ships could not go much faster than 15 knots. But in the landlocked waters of the Baltic, within one or two hours it could have moved into the shelter of a bay and from our point of view the situation would have changed completely. That is why it is so important to have the most up-to-date information possible on the position of the force.'

Kormoran is at its most effective against ships in open water, where there is no risk of radar echoes from land nearby seducing the missiles away from their intended targets. When engaging ships close to the coast or in harbour, the Tornadoes would attack with normal general-purpose bombs. So a force equipped to attack shipping in open water might have difficulty in mounting an effective attack against ships close to the coast.

A further problem facing an air commander trying to attack ships at sea is that he has little choice over the time of day or the weather conditions in which his forces launch their attack. The enemy naval commander would choose where he sent his ships and when, he would make as much use as possible of shore cover, and when he exposed his force to air attack it would be on the best possible terms from his point of view. Thus the Germany Navy Tornadoes would not be able to choose to attack the enemy ships only at night as they might wish; they would have to mount the best attack they could, by day or by night, against a fleeting target as soon as possible after it had presented itself.

Typically, an anti-shipping attack flight would comprise six Tornadoes. If sent off at night, the aircraft would fly individual routes to their attack positions. If sent by day, the aircraft would stay together for mutual support so that if necessary they could fight their way through enemy fighter patrols covering the ships, using their Sidewinder missiles. Any attack plan would have to take enemy fighter cover into consideration: if a naval force was important enough to warrant attack, the enemy would almost certainly consider it important enough to require such a defence.

On nearing the enemy convoy the Tornado formation would split up and aircraft would move individually to their missile launch positions in accordance with a pre-arranged plan. The aim would be to launch the first salvo of missiles at the ships simultaneously and from several different directions, to achieve maximum surprise, concentration and shock effect:

'With its very exact navigation system the Tornado can fly to a given point precisely, to within less than a second. So we can arrange for all of the aircraft to arrive at assigned points at exactly the same time. The idea is for the aircraft to launch their missiles simultaneously from many different directions, to saturate the defences around the enemy force.'

As well as providing a most difficult problem for the defenders, having the aircraft launch their attacks from separate assigned sectors prevents aircraft getting in each other's way during missile launch, and it reduces the chances of more than one aircraft aiming its missiles at any one ship.

During the final moments of such an attack things would happen very quickly:

'The Tornadoes would run in singly towards their assigned

missile launch points, keeping below the enemy radar cover. We would use the Kormoran's stand-off capability to its fullest extent and fire the missiles at their maximum possible range. When the WSO estimated that his aircraft was within Kormoran range of the target he would switch on his radar and the enemy force should appear on his screen. If it did not, the pilot might have to climb the aircraft a little until the ships did appear.'

If the target was a large escorted convoy it might be necessary for the aircraft to launch their first salvo of missiles at some of the warships around its periphery, to neutralize these ships and allow the aircraft to get close enough to the centre of the force to attack the high-value targets there. Having selected his first target, the WSO would place an electronic marker over its blip on the radar screen, press a button to lock the target into the attack computer, then make the switches to prepare the missile for launch. Several seconds after launching its first missile each aircraft would launch its second, turn tightly through a semi-circle, then withdraw at high speed. Provided the Tornadoes kept more than ten miles from the escorting warships and stayed low, they would be safe from enemy suface-to-air missiles. To guide a missile on to an aircraft and knock it down, a ship's missile operators would need to be able to lock their fire-control radar on to the aircraft for at least a minute (the missile would need much of that time to cover the distance). Normally the Tornadoes would not expose themselves above the radar horizon for anything like that length of time.

The time of flight of a Kormoran missile, from launch at maximum range to impact, is about two minutes. Throughout this time the enemy convoy would be in the thoroughly discomforting position of having a dozen missiles streaking towards it at low altitude and high speed, from several points on the compass. Even though some of the ships might be able to deflect missiles using electronic countermeasures, there is a high probability that several of the missiles would score hits. (During the Falklands War the container ship *Atlantic Conveyor* was struck by a missile deflected away from one of the escorting warships.) If the convoy was large enough it might be subjected to repeated Kormoran attacks by forces of Tornadoes and F-104s, followed up by bomb attacks against the survivors trying to reach positions of safety close to the coast:

'Ships hit by Kormoran will usually be left immobile with their fire control radars knocked out, at least for a while. If required, such ships could be finished off in later attacks using 'dumb' bombs.'

A Kormoran attack of the type described is an example of modern warfare at its most impersonal: none of the aircrew would get within visual range of the ships they were attacking. Targets would be selected by the size of their radar echo and their position within the force, neither of which would provide an infallible means of identification: a small ship side-on gives a larger radar echo than a large ship end-on. Once hostilities had begun, the waters of the Baltic would be an extremely dangerous place for surface ships, whether or not they were combatants.

The recent conflict in the South Atlantic brought to the fore the effectiveness of sea-skimming missiles against surface ships. Did the conflict hold any lessons for the German naval air attack units?

'The lessons from the Falklands War are for the surface warships rather than for us. The success of the Argentine air-launched Exocets has convinced people that in Kormoran we have the right sort of weapon, but we in the Marine Flieger Geschwader knew that before the conflict. The people on our surface ships learned a lot from the British experience. During our German national exercises, and NATO exercises, we gave our surface warships the opportunity to try to counter our type of attack. The handling of surface ships, their sea-skimming missile defence procedures and tactics, have improved quite a bit.'

Having visited MFG 1 and had a chance to gauge its effectiveness, this author has no doubt that if the Argentine Navy had been able to deploy a comparable force, the Falklands conflict would have had an entirely different outcome.

In time of war the two German Marine Flieger Geschwader would exert considerable influence on the course of naval operations in the Baltic. But, like other commanders inter-viewed, Volke Liche did not think such a conflict likely:

'I do not think a war in Central Europe is likely, as long as the situation remains balanced as it is now, because I do not think either side has idiots in charge of it. I do not agree with the Soviet system, but I believe they are proud of what they have achieved. They have different ideas of what to be proud of than we have. I cannot imagine that they would willingly risk everything they have achieved in the last sixty years, by starting an all-out war against the West. The Soviets have shown that they are prepared to use force to expand their influence in the world, but only where they feel they can do so without undue risk to themselves.

I think that in NATO our main task is to convince the other side that they cannot possibly win a war against us easily. So we have to demonstrate that our forces are combat-ready at all times. Only if we ceased to demonstrate that might a war become a serious possibility.'

15: Protecting the Lifeline

The commander of No. 11 Group, responsible for the air defence of the United Kingdom and the surrounding sea areas, is Air Vice Marshal Ken Hayr who came from New Zealand to join the Royal Air Force in 1954. After gaining his wings he completed two tours on Hunters and one on Lightnings, served at the Central Fighter Establishment and was then a squadron commander at the Phantom Operational Conversion Unit. In 1970 he took command of No. 1 Squadron, the first unit to receive Harriers, and was responsible for the service introduction of this revolutionary new aircraft. After promotion to Group Captain he commanded the fighter base at Binbrook in Lincolnshire, operating Lightnings. He held further staff appointments and during the Falklands conflict in 1982 was Assistant Chief of Air Staff (operations) at the Ministry of Defence in London. He took up his present appointment in August 1982.

Any description of the air defence of the United Kingdom must invite comparison with the operations by RAF Fighter Command during the Battle of Britain in 1940. Ken Hayr has a keen sense of history and his headquarters at Bentley Priory is only about a hundred yards from the building where Sir Hugh Dowding directed the battle. In many ways Ken Hayr's position is similar to Dowding's during the late 1930s, when the latter built up his system of fighter control which made use of the latest developments in radar and communications technology. Today Britain's air defences are mid-way through a series of changes that will be almost as far-reaching, with the introduction of high-technology ground and airborne radars and computer-based data transmission and analysis systems:

'The threat to the United Kingdom, having been re-identified in the 1970s, called for a major strengthening of our air defences. Thus my position is similar to that of Air Marshal Dowding who had to build up Fighter Command during the late 1930s. God forbid that in the end we shall prove to have been right in expanding, through being tested in conflict, as Dowding was. As well as introducing new fighters, Dowding integrated his new radars with a system of communications to form the fighter control system that was to prove crucially important during the Battle of Britain. Today Britain's air defences are in a similar state of transition, both in the air and on the ground, and I am as involved as Dowding was in bringing together the threads of the new system.'

Ken Hayr began by describing the sort of targets in the United Kingdom which an enemy might be expected to attack and which No. 11 Group was responsible for defending:

'As a base for British and American nuclear weapons, the United Kingdom is of strategic importance in its own right. In addition the United Kingdom is vitally important to NATO as a reinforcing base. The country has been described as a huge, unsinkable aircraft carrier and most reinforcements to Europe from the USA would come either via Britain or through the airspace or seaspace surrounding it.

No. 11 Group is also responsible for the protection of maritime forces operating in the North Sea or in the northeast Atlantic. In fact we would not attempt to discriminate between enemy aircraft attacking land targets and those attacking ships at sea, because it would usually be impossible to tell which targets were being singled out before missile launch.

In a war I would expect an enemy to try to hit United Kingdom airfields and ports involved in moving troops, equipment and supplies to the continent of Europe or receiving them from the USA. These would be lucrative targets, especially the airfields where there would be large numbers of chartered civil aircraft and military transports taking off and landing.'

The *meetable* threat to the United Kingdom and nearby

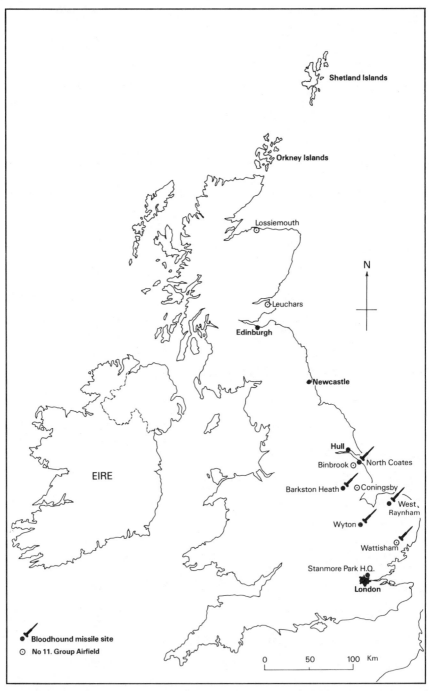

No. 11 Group Royal Air Force, main airfields and surface-to-air missile sites

shipping which No. 11 Group is expected to counter is from manned aircraft carrying either free-fall bombs or cruise missiles. No. 11 Group possesses no anti-ballistic missile defence system, so it can do nothing to prevent ballstic missiles reaching the United Kingdom, though it does control the Ballistic Missile Warning System radars at Fylingdales which would provide warning of their approach. The sole deterrent to ballistic missile attack is the threat of a retaliatory counter-strike.

'The manned aircraft threat is from Soviet Backfire, Badger and Blinder bombers attacking from the north, east and west, and Fencer fighter-bombers coming from the east. There is also a threat from cruise missiles which could come from any direction. Cruise missiles fly relatively slowly, at about .8 Mach, but their small size makes them difficult to track and intercept.'

To be successful, an air defence system must have adequate radar warning of the approach of enemy aircraft. Currently No. 11 Group's ground radar chain is being re-equipped with modern high-technology radars which, to render them less vulnerable to attack, are not committed to fixed sites as were their predecessors. Two types of mobile long-range radar are being introduced: the British Martello and the American Type 592. A third new radar, the British Plessey AR320, has been ordered. All three radars have flat-plate antenna systems and employ the latest techniques to provide a three-dimensional picture of the air situation:

'The United Kingdom ground radar chain, which at present is our primary means of recognizing incoming attacks and reacting to them, is being re-equipped with new types of radar. Previously our air defence radars have all been at fixed sites whose positions are known to potential enemies and could be targeted accurately. The new radars coming into service are mobile, so we can move them between different sites to conceal their positions. In addition we have refurbished our underground air defence bunkers, giving them increased protection from attack. The radar picture from the mobile sets will be transmitted to these bunkers via satellite, radio or landline data links.'

In time of war the air defence radars could come under attack from aircraft dropping conventional free-fall bombs, from radar-homing missiles or from electronic jamming. Ken Hayr outlined the ways in which modern radar technology is used to make an attacker's task more difficult:

'Moving the radars around from time to time would certainly make them less vulnerable to attack from conventional bombers. Radiation-homing missiles pose a severe threat: it is relatively easy to design a weapon which will home on a radar's transmissions, and even if radars were moved around they would still have to emit. But we could control the frequencies, the type and the timing of the emissions to make it harder for a missile to home on the radar itself. There is also a good chance that a modern radar would see a missile coming in time to switch off, and so leave the missile with no emissions on which to home. So there are several tactics we could play to make our radars less vulnerable to this type of attack. In addition, to make electronic jamming difficult, the new radars are able to switch rapidly between frequencies and they employ a full range of counter-countermeasures systems.

Of course, these new radars would not provide much warning of aircraft or cruise missiles coming in at low level, because we are stuck with the law of physics which states that normal radar transmissions move only in straight lines and cannot see beneath the horizon.'

For long-range warning of aircraft or missiles approaching at low altitudes No. 11 Group uses radar information from airborne early warning (AEW) aircraft such as the elderly Shackleton and the Boeing E-3A AWACS. From 20,000 feet the radar from the latter can see low-flying aircraft anywhere in a circle of airspace 400 miles in diameter, and just three of these aircraft on patrol at any one time could cover all the main axes of threat to the United Kingdom. Also, if enemy aircraft were to come from bases in East Germany or Poland, continental radar stations would provide warning of their approach.

In 1940 Sir Hugh Dowding's system of air defence was a major advance on what had gone before, not only because it employed radar to plot the movement of enemy aircraft, but also because it provided for the information to be filtered and passed to those who were to use it. Today Ken Hayr and his staff are involved in a continuing programme to improve the processing of air defence information:

'Using modern micro-electronics to integrate information channelled in from all of our surface and airborne early warning radars, we now compile a very refined master air defence picture which shows what is happening. In 1940 Dowding stood on a balcony at his headquarters looking down on a map of the United Kingdom measuring about 20 feet by 10 feet, on which WAAF plotters moved counters. Today I have a screen about the size of that of a home television on which I receive an air defence picture covering an area similar to Dowding's, or as much of it as I want. At my headquarters I can see on my screen the same radar picture as my fighter controllers or sector commanders are seeing. It is as though I were looking over their shoulders, though there could be hundreds of miles between us. The master air defence picture is put into a 'ring-main' running round the country, so that any part of the air defence system can draw out the information it wants.

A further advantage of this new technique is that we can produce a simulation of the total system. We can write a computer programme for an air defence battle and run it on the screens to see how we would cope with various types of attack. Afterwards we can replay the whole thing and say, 'That's where we made the mistake . . .' If mistakes are made we can pinpoint the reasons and learn from them.'

All modern air defence commanders face problems in distinguishing hostile aircraft from friendly ones before missiles are launched. Without a reliable system of electronic identification, long-range surface-to-air and air-to-air missiles cannot be used to anything like their full capability. If an aircraft was adhering to a previously assigned flight plan and was seen to be radiating the correct IFF coded reply signal for a given time period, that would establish it as friendly. The problem comes when large numbers of aircraft are present in the same area and the identification system becomes overloaded. Then fighters might have to be sent to carry out visual identifications:

'Identification is a major problem, because before we launched a missile at an aircraft we would have to be sure that it was hostile. With the large number of aircraft that would be flying between the United Kingdom and the continent of Europe during a conflict, we could very quickly exhaust our fighter defence force in carrying out visual identifications on aircraft which subsequently turned out to be friendly – or else perhaps shoot some of them down. We can't afford that.

We are looking for a much better IFF system than the one we have at present. A lot of work is being done and a lot of money is to be spent in producing a reliable electronic IFF system. But we have not cracked the problem yet. I believe that the technology exists to produce a combined system employing information from different sensors which would give a high level of confidence that a blip seen on radar was hostile. Once we had that knowledge our fighters and surface-to-air missile batteries could engage targets to the full capability of their weapons. But whatever is devised has to be resistant to jamming; and it must not allow enemy aircraft to sample the coded reply signals and re-radiate them in such a way that they would appear as 'friendlies'. If it could be made to work, the system would have to be fitted to aircraft throughout NATO and that would mean buying an enormous amount of equipment. This is one area where we would have to have commonality – all NATO air forces must work to a common IFF system.'

To protect the area assigned to it, No. 11 Group's fighter force currently comprises the equivalent of six squadrons of Phantoms and three of Lightnings (including aircraft and pilots from the operational conversion unit for each type). In addition there are the equivalent of three squadrons of Hawk trainers operating in the day fighter role. In time of conflict No. 11 Group might be augmented by a few squadrons of F-15s and F-16s from the USA, though their numbers would be far smaller than those earmarked for Central Europe.

From time to time NATO aircraft carriers and warships with long-range surface-to-air missile systems could be expected to provide a useful stiffening of No. 11 Group's resources:

'If US or Royal Navy aircraft carriers came into the sea areas around the UK, their aircraft would be integrated into the air defence system and used to engage targets. Naturally we would have to ensure that our respective aircraft did not get in each other's way and there was no risk of their shooting each other down. Warships in the area equipped with long-range surface-to-air missiles would also form part of our integrated air defence.'

Currently the backbone of No. 11 Group's fighter force, the two-seat McDonnell Douglas Phantom has been in service with the RAF for some fifteen years and is beginning to show its age. This aircraft has characteristics similar to those of the RF-4C described in Chapter 10. In the air defence role the Royal Air Force Phantoms carry an armament of four Skyflash radar semi-active missiles (similar in capability to the AIM-7F Sparrow missiles carried by the F-15 and described in Chapter 3) and four AIM-9L Sidewinder infra-red homing missiles, plus a 20 mm cannon in an underfuselage pod. For the long-range all-weather interceptor role, the Phantom has a very good speed and range performance, and its long-range pulse-doppler radar is able to distinguish low-flying aircraft against a background of ground or sea clutter.

The single-seat twin-engined British Aerospace Lightning is even older than the Phantom and dates from the late 1950s; in its combat configuration the Lightning has a take-off weight of about 22 tons. Although it has supersonic performance and is still an effective night and all-weather interceptor at high altitude, the Lightning's obsolete pulsed radar has a poor capability against aircraft flying low over land; and the two outdated Firestreak or Red Top infra-red homing missiles it carries, supplemented by two 30 mm cannon, give it considerably less fire power than the Phantom. The Lightning is due to be phased out of service in 1988.

One recent addition to No. 11 Group's order of battle in time of war is the equivalent of three squadrons of British Aerospace Hawks, an additional seventy-two aircraft. The Hawk is a two-seat, single-engined advanced trainer with a maximum speed at low altitude of about 540 knots. In the combat role the aircraft would carry two AIM-9L Sidewinder missiles and would be flown as a single-seater by instructor pilots; in this configuration the Hawk would have a take-off weight of about 5½ tons. This move reflects the RAF's intention in war to make the maximum possible use of every type of aircraft in service. Compared with the Phantom or Lightning, the Hawk lacks radar and is able to carry out interceptions only by day and in clear skies. Is the fighting capability it brings really worth even the limited cost of securing it?

'It is not just a cynical approach to think that way. But in this case the practice outweighs the theory. First of all, I would point out that in most respects the Hawk's performance is comparable with that of the Sea Harrier which operated so effectively as an air defence fighter during the Falklands conflict. Moreover, it carries the same type of air-to-air missile, the AIM-9L Sidewinder. However, the real value of the Hawk lies in its high turning performance. If he is positioned ahead of the enemy formation by ground radar, an AEW aircraft or even a Phantom, a Hawk pilot with his target in visual contact can turn so quicky that he can attack with Sidewinders before the enemy aircraft – whatever its speed – can get past him. In time of war No. 11 Group would use quite a number of Hawks. The real value of this agile and aggressive little aeroplane has been amply demonstrated in air defence exercises.'

At the time of writing, the Panavia Tornado F2 has just entered service and a training unit has been formed within No. 11 Group. This aircraft is the long-range night and all-weather interceptor version of the two-seat twin-engined swing-wing Tornado GR1 described in Chapter 6, and differs from the attack version in that the fuselage is slightly longer and accommodates more fuel, and its radar and many of its avionic systems are designed for air-to-air combat rather than air-to-ground operations. The Tornado F3 with more powerful engines and detailed internal changes will be the main production version of this aircraft, and is scheduled to replace all Lightnings and most Phantoms in No. 11 Group during the late 1980s.

At a first glance at the brochure figures, the Tornado F3 might seem to offer only small advances over the Phantom. At high altitude the new fighter is little faster than its predecessor; against a large aircraft the Phantom's radar's maximum target pick-up range is not much short of that of the Tornado's AI 24 radar; and initially both aircraft will carry the same missile armament. In assessing the relative fighting value of the Tornado compared with its predecessor, other yardsticks have to be used. For the late 1980s a fighter defending the United Kingdom requires a high maximum speed *at low altitude*, a long endurance and a radar that is reliable and able to pick up small targets – such as cruise missiles – at great distances. And in these respects the Tornado F3 is a considerable improvement over the Phantom. The Tornado carries almost exactly the same internal fuel as the Phantom, but its engines are of later design and fuel consumption in normal flight is about one-third less. So the new fighter will have sufficient fuel to fly normal missions without carrying external fuel tanks, and this gives it an important advantage: during high-speed flight a lot of fuel has to be burned merely to overcome the drag of external tanks. The Tornado F3 will carry such tanks only for ferry flights or patrols far from base. The fact that the Tornado's cannon is mounted internally, rather than in a draggy external pod, also helps to improve aerodynamic cleanliness. Together these factors will reduce the need for pilots to use reheat in combat, with a further reduction in the rate of fuel consumption:

'The Tornado is 'slippery' at low altitude, it accelerates very quickly and if bunted from 5,000 feet it will go supersonic in cold power [i.e. without using reheat]. In a similar situation a Phantom pilot would have to use reheat.

Moreover, the Tornado will be able to remain on patrol much further from its base than a Phantom without recourse to air-to-air refuelling; or, looking at it another way, the Tornado will be able to spend about twice as long on patrol at the same distance out. This is important because we need to be able to intercept enemy aircraft before they can launch air-to-surface missiles against land targets or shipping.

The Tornado's radar will not necessarily see aircraft at much greater ranges than a Phantom's, but its technology is later by a generation and will allow the crew to track multiple targets almost simultaneously. The Phantom's radar has a good long-range performance when it works well, but it requires a lot of maintenance. More importantly, against small targets like cruise missiles the new radar should be considerably more effective than its predecessor.'

The swing-wing Tornado takes off and lands more slowly than other supersonic fighters; and after landing the aircraft's built-in thrust-reversal system greatly reduces the landing run, especially on wet runways. As a result the Tornado F3 will be able to conduct routine operations from short runways that are unsuitable for other types of high-speed aircraft:

'With its wings swept forward, the take-off speed for a combat-loaded Tornado is about 150 knots, compared with 180 knots for a Phantom. And using reverse thrust after landing the Tornado can stop within 700 yards, even with no wind and a wet runway, compared with 2,000 yards for a Phantom. This means that Tornadoes will be able to operate from 1,500-yard runways compared with the 2,500 yards which is the norm for the Phantom. Once the Tornado F3 is in service I can see us basing the aircraft forward, even as far north as the Shetlands if required.'

Providing a second line of defence behind the fighters, No. 11 Group has two squadrons of British Aerospace Bloodhound long-range surface-to-air missiles operating from six sites in

Lincolnshire, Norfolk, Suffolk and Huntingdonshire to protect likely targets in eastern England. Like the Phantom, the Bloodhound missile system is getting rather long-in-the-tooth though it still poses a formidable obstacle to enemy aircraft. The much newer but smaller and shorter-range British Aerospace Rapier surface-to-air missile provides point defence at some of the more important airfields. In addition, a unit has recently been formed in No. 11 Group to operate several fast-firing 35 mm Oerlikon anti-aircraft guns captured from the Argentine forces on the Falklands, also in the point-defence role:

'Bloodhound represents an extra string to the air defence bow which I regard very highly. However, it has to be integrated with the rest of the system. With Bloodhound, as with fighters, the ability to distinguish between hostile and friendly aircraft is crucially important: you need to be certain you are attacking an enemy aircraft rather than a friendly one. In common with the rest of the UK air defence system, we are seeking ways of enhancing the effectiveness of Bloodhound and improving its command and control system.

So you can see that the air defence of the United Kingdom is made up of several layers. The Phantoms, Lightnings and Hawks provide the first layer, well out to sea. Bloodhound provides the next layer. Hawks on visual patrol over land provide the next and, finally, there are the Rapier and anti-aircraft gun batteries.'

Having outlined the composition of his force and some of the ways in which it would be used in war, Ken Hayr expressed confidence in the ability of No. 11 Group to deal with any attack on the United Kingdom by manned aircraft or cruise missiles. His force has the advantage that enemy aircraft approaching the United Kingdom would have to come in over the sea, which would make the interception less difficult than if they approached over land:

'No. 11 Group has the advantage of being able to intercept aircraft over the sea, and we should benefit from notification of the approach of some enemy aircraft from radars on the

Continent. In Germany, air defence has much more immedia-cy about it than ours. United Kingdom air defence is a management challenge rather than a case of shooting from the hip – which would tend to be the outcome in the central region of Europe. On the other hand, the area I have to defend is much larger than that of the air commanders on the Conti-nent. I therefore have to make full use of the mobility and flexibility that is unique to air power. For example, one of my Phantoms could be flying an air defence patrol over shipping off Denmark on one sortie, doing the same thing off the south of Ireland on the next and carrying out an interception off the north of the Shetlands on the one after that.

That is why we continue to rely on fighter aircraft: they still offer the most flexible and reliable means of combating other aircraft. Only the manned interceptor can engage enemy aircraft at long range before they can launch their air-to-surface missiles at targets. And there is the ever-present problem of identification: unless we can be absolutely sure of the identity of an aircraft, the human presence on the scene is still the most reliable IFF system we have.

In a conventional war an enemy cannot continue making air attacks if he loses more than a certain percentage of his force on each wave. From what we have seen on exercises, we would be able to achieve that level of attrition.'

16: Air Battle Central Europe: An Overview

In the preceding chapters we have examined several of the types of air operation which might take place over and around a land battle in Central Europe if it were fought in the 1980s. The purpose of this chapter is to give an overview of the air battle in the light of what the interviewees have said, to discuss aspects not covered during the interviews, and to draw together some lessons on the nature of modern air warfare.

The defensive counter-air battle

Two distinct types of defensive counter-air battle were discussed during the interviews. Air Marshal Hine (Chapter 1) and Major Casey (Chapter 3) described the 'shoot-from-the-hip' air superiority battle that would be fought over Central Europe, which would include numerous air-to-air combats between opposing fighters. Air Vice Marshal Hayr (Chapter 15) described the quite different type of operation to defend the United Kingdom and the surrounding sea areas from attack by manned aircraft and cruise missiles; this would be fought mainly over the sea by long-range fighters supported by tanker aircraft, usually against unescorted bombers and missile launching aircraft. In each case the defenders would be assisted by airborne warning and control aircraft overseeing the air battle from vantage points safely clear of it.

During these defensive counter-air battles the fighters would co-ordinate their operations with those of medium-range and long-range surface-to-air missiles: Hawk and Nike batteries in western Germany, Bloodhound batteries in eastern England. In addition there would be short-range anti-aircraft missiles and guns providing point defence around individual targets. In general, the fighters would engage enemy aircraft in front of and behind the missile engagement zones.

Surface-to-air missiles can be deadly against aircraft flying at medium or high altitude. But despite exaggerated claims made for their effectiveness, recent wars have shown them to be much less dangerous against aircraft flying at low altitude and making good use of terrain. If the attack aircraft carry self-protection electronic countermeasures, or are accompanied by 'Wild Weasel' or jamming escort aircraft, the effectiveness of the missiles is further reduced. When over hostile territory attack aircraft will usually pick their way between areas of known defences at low altitude, thus giving surface-to-air missile and gun batteries only fleeting opportunities to engage. Such fixed defences cannot exercise initiative in the air battle; they have to wait until enemy aircraft choose to pass, or happen to blunder, within their reach.

Although surface-to-air missiles would probably inflict serious losses on occasions, there is little doubt that in any major conflict in Europe the air defence fighters would be the real killers. Fighters and surface-to-air missiles are different but essential ingredients of an air defence system, however, and should not be thought of as competing systems: surface-to-air missiles limit the freedom of operation of attack aircraft over the ground; and by forcing enemy aircraft to operate at low level, the missiles deprive them of freedom of movement in the vertical plane and effectively restrict them to two-dimensional operations.

A major constraint on defensive counter-air operations, and in particular on the use of long-range surface-to-air and air-to-air missile systems to engage targets at beyond visual range, is the difficulty of establishing positively whether an aircraft tracked on radar is friendly or hostile. Failure to do so effectively could place a missile operator on the horns of an uncomfortable dilemma: to withhold fire, in which case possible enemy aircraft would be allowed to go about their tasks unhindered; or engage and risk 'fratricide'. Fratricide is doubly wasteful: as well as causing the unnecessary loss of valuable crews and combat aircraft, it diverts the attention of defending fighters and missile batteries away from the enemy aircraft that they should be engaging.

The current NATO electronic IFF (Identification Friend or

Foe) system employs interrogator transmitters on the ground or in fighter or AWACS aircraft which, in effect, ask aircraft in their areas, 'Are you friendly?' The IFF transponder in each friendly aircraft should then reply with a coded signal saying 'I am friendly' and the interrogator will receive and decode these signals. If the system worked perfectly those aircraft which did not give the correct reply could then be regarded as hostile, and treated accordingly. Unfortunately, however, the system does not work perfectly. Just because an interrogator does not see a correct reply signal from an aircraft, it does not necessarily mean that aircraft is hostile. Modern IFF transponders are very reliable, but during a conflict some will go unserviceable or incur battle damage, thereby preventing a friendly aircraft transmitting a reply. And even if a correct reply was being transmitted, it might not be recognized. During an all-out air battle over Central Europe there might be several hundred friendly aircraft within a relatively small volume of sky, all of which would return 'I am friendly' signals when triggered by each of the scores of interrogators which might be in the same area. The deluge of replies could cause electronic 'traffic jams' at some of the interrogators, making it impossible to distinguish between those aircraft which had replied and those which had not.

A partial answer to the identification problem is very careful management of airspace over friendly territory, to keep track of the movements of friendly attack aircraft passing to and from their targets. But although the provision of reliable electronic identification for aircraft is a high-priority NATO requirement receiving vigorous attention from industry, the problem is likely to haunt air commanders well into the 1990s. The only consolation is that the Warsaw Pact air forces face a similar problem, made worse by the fact that they have many more aircraft and their electronic systems are less advanced than their Western counterparts'.

Offensive counter-air operations

Air Marshal Hine (Chapter 1) and Wing Commander McLeod (Chapter 6) described the concept behind offensive counter-air attacks on enemy airfields. A modern hardened military airfield is difficult to put out of action even for a short time. To do so would require co-ordinated attacks on headquarters bunkers, fuel and weapons storage areas, runways and taxiways, delivered by aircraft which would in many cases have to pass within range of defending surface-to-air missile and gun batteries. On their side, the attackers have the advantage that they would hold the initiative and could exploit three of the great attributes of air power: surprise, concentration and shock action. Surprise and concentration depend on careful preparation, and if these can be achieved the shock effect will usually follow. Airfields are static targets and it is reasonable to suppose that all important ones would have been photographed from satellites long before the outbreak of any conflict. Their positions, layouts and surrounding areas would thus be known and planning staffs can draw up highly detailed plans for set-piece co-ordinated attacks. Attacking forces would choose their routes carefully to allow the defences minimum time to react and could strike at night or in bad weather, or during periods of both, when the defences would be at their least effective.

Airfields would be the main offensive counter-air targets but not the only ones. Air defence command bunkers, air defence radars, surface-to-air missile batteries and air force support facilities also come under this category and those likely to have a bearing on the land–air battle would come under attack.

Battlefield air support operations: general

Air power is able to exert unique pressures on the land battle. Attack aircraft can take off from widely separated bases, concentrate rapidly and simultaneously on selected targets far behind the battle area and put down enormous destructive power with great accuracy. A few hours later those same aircraft could be hitting quite different targets situated many scores of miles away from the first. Modern reconnaissance aircraft can observe and record virtually everything happening on the ground in the enemy rear areas, by day or by night. These are valuable attributes that cannot be matched by surface-bound systems.

By its nature air power is extremely flexible, able to perform many different tasks in a host of different ways. But because of this virtue some of its limitations often pass unrecognized. There are some tasks which, although they can be carried out effectively by specialized aircraft or by aircraft carrying specialized weapons, do not represent a cost-effective option for normal aircraft carrying general-purpose bombs. Examples of this are close air support operations against individual tanks by A-10 attack aircraft, and attacks on bridges by the F-111Fs carrying laser-guided bombs. In each case these aircraft would succeed by virtue of their specialized features, when similar attacks by non-specialized aircraft would require an excessive number of sorties to achieve the same results. Thus effective air attack operations depend to a large extent on skilful matching of each type of aircraft to its optimum range of targets.

Moreover, in order to understand the ways in which air power would best be used to support the land battle, it is necessary to pay heed to those things which aircraft cannot do well or which can be done better or more cheaply by other systems. For example, it is a misuse of attack aircraft to use them to perform tasks that can be done by artillery. If there are sufficient guns or rocket launchers within range of the target and its location is known, these can engage far more rapidly than can aircraft, do so with greater accuracy, sustain fire over far longer periods and concentrate a greater volume of fire. If artillery weapons are in position to perform a given destructive task, they will usually do it more cost-effectively than can aircraft.

Air attacks can be very effective against ground forces on the move, either advancing or pulling back; such forces will tend to concentrate at points along their route, and when they do they will be vulnerable to air attack. Air attacks are considerably less effective against ground forces dispersed in camouflaged positions, which are difficult to locate from the air and do not usually make cost-effective targets.

Battlefield air support operations: interdiction

During most phases of the land battle high-speed attack aircraft would give their most effective support by mounting interdiction operations, to disrupt the movement of enemy troops and supplies to the battle area. There are two main ways of doing this: by attacking the road and rail systems to the battle area, and by attacking the troops and supplies being moved. Interdiction missions divide further into battlefield air interdiction missions, those against targets in the narrow band just behind the battle area, and deep interdiction missions against targets further back.

In an area like Central Europe where there are several major rivers, the destruction of bridges could be a rewarding part of any attack on the enemy transport system. In the past, however, such a requirement was far easier to state than to achieve. Major bridges are usually strongly built, and bridges of military importance would invariably be well defended. In previous wars, bridges have proved particularly difficult targets for air attack, and some of the most gallant and costly failures in the history of aerial warfare have been during attacks on heavily defended bridges whose destruction was deemed crucial to the land battle. Nowadays, the destruction of bridges would usually be the task of specially trained crews, using precision attack weapons like the laser-guided Paveway described by Lieutenant-Colonel Fazackerley (Chapter 5). Against such targets a combination of operator skill and high-technology weaponry promises to succeed where bravery and determination failed in the past.

The attack on troops, vehicles and supplies moving up to the battle area would occupy 2 ATAF's short-range high-speed attack force for most of the conflict. By day, forces of a dozen or more Harrier, Alphajet, Mirage, F-16 and NF-5 aircraft, in some cases supported by radar-jamming EF-111s and 'Wild Weasel' F-4Gs, would be sent to attack concentrations of enemy vehicles located behind the battle area. To attack enemy vehicle concentrations by night would require a more complex weapon system, such as the Tornado carrying the MW-1 area attack weapon and described by Oberstleutnant Jertz (Chapter 7).

Although a vigorous interdiction campaign could cause considerable disruption to the movement of enemy forces, in areas where there is plenty of natural cover it would be unrealistic to expect a complete severance of the enemy supply lines. Unless they have recourse to nuclear weapons, aircraft cannot deny ground to an enemy for any length of time or halt movement completely.

Battlefield air support: close air support

Close air support operations are those mounted against targets near friendly forces. To prevent such attacks falling on the very troops they were supposed to support, the attacking aircraft would have to be directed on to their targets by forward air controllers on the ground or in helicopters.

Close air support operations which involve brief forays over enemy-held territory would best be made by purpose-designed, medium-speed armoured attack aircraft, like the A-10 described by Lieutenant-Colonel Lyon (Chapter 9). In fact the A-10 is so specialized a design that in Europe it would probably be used for nothing else but close air support. The A-10s would spend most of their time at orbit points over friendly territory just behind the battle area. Directed by a forward air controller, they would make snap attacks, penetrating no more than about five miles into enemy territory, before returning to their orbit points until the next target was found for them. Deeper penetrations into enemy-held territory would risk encountering the heavier types of anti-aircraft weapon, which could defeat the armour of the A-10 and which the aircraft lacks the speed to avoid.

Another effective form of close air support would be provided by anti-tank helicopters, like the Lynx described by Lieutenant-Colonel Hyde-Smith (Chapter 11). Although these helicopters could be very effective in this role, however, they are extremely vulnerable to return fire and could engage only from positions clear of enemy ground forces.

In terms of the number of enemy vehicles destroyed for sorties flown, high-speed jet aircraft are likely to be far more effective flying interdiction missions rather than close air support missions. The only time fast jets would be suitable for close air support would be if there were concentrations of enemy vehicles in the battle area during an attack or following a break-through.

Then pilots would have little difficultly in finding targets worth attacking and it would not be difficult to distinguish enemy forces from friendly ones.

Tactical reconnaissance

Regular tactical reconnaissance is vitally important if offensive air operations are to be mounted successfully: the more that can be known about a target, the more carefully an attack can be planned and the more effective it is likely to be. Such reconnaissance could come from specialized aircraft like the RF-4C described by Lieutenant-Colonel Loveland (Chapter 10), from attack aircraft used in the visual reconnaissance role, from short-range unmanned drones or from debriefing reports from crews of attack aircraft returning from enemy territory. The information thus received would be collated with that from satellite, electronic and other intelligence sources, to build up the most detailed picture possible of what the enemy was doing.

Modern aerial reconnaissance employs a spread of sensors which includes optical and infra-red cameras, infra-red recording systems and electronic reconnaissance equipment. In a fast-moving land battle, however, visual reconnaissance reports passed by radio still have an important place: modern technology has yet to put in service a method that can get vital reconnaissance information to its users faster than this.

In each type of attack operation against land targets described in this book, it is vitally important to separate the reconnaissance task from the attack task even if aircraft of the same type perform both roles. The so-called 'armed reconnaissance' (also called 'search and destroy') mission implies that aircraft are sent out in ones and twos to locate their own targets which they then attack. Such attacks are unlikely to achieve surprise, since the aircraft will have flown past the target shortly before; and one or two aircraft would usually not be sufficient to deliver a concentrated attack on a target of importance. Thus aircraft engaged in armed reconnaissance forgo two of the great advantages of air power in attack: surprise and concentration of force. Bitter experience during several wars has shown that if such missions are flown in defended areas they are liable to suffer losses out of all proportion to the damage they inflict on the enemy.

Anti-shipping operations

Although air power cannot hold ground or deny it completely to an enemy, the history of air warfare provides many examples where the vigorous application of air power has denied an enemy the effective use of the surface of the sea. This is the role of the German Navy Tornado force as described by Fregattenkapitaen Liche (Chapter 14). Ships traversing areas of sea cannot avoid being observed on radar, and the Falklands conflict demonstrated their vulnerability to air-launched, sea-skimming radar-homing missiles. Hits on even a few transports could disrupt an amphibious landing operation completely, and however well the ships were escorted it would be impossible to guarantee that none of the sea-skimmers would get through. Without doubt the presence of the German Navy's anti-shipping Tornadoes would be a major factor inhibiting the movement of Warsaw Pact shipping through the Baltic in time of conflict.

Air transport

Although transport aircraft would play no direct role in a land – air battle in Central Europe, their indirect role in moving forces and equipment into and around the war zone would be vitally important to the success of every form of military operation. To supplement military transport aircraft, large numbers of civilian airliners and cargo aircraft would be pressed into use to move reinforcements from the USA and Great Britain into Western Europe.

The type of military air transport operation that most captures the imagination is the airborne assault to seize territory held by the enemy. These are spectacular affairs, involving large formations of paratroop-carrying aircraft or transport helicopters disgorging hundreds of assault troops and their weapons straight into action. Although there would certainly be a place for airborne assaults of this type during a land battle in Central Europe, most air transport operations in support of such a conflict would be far less spectacular.

During military airlift operations, aircraft fly singly at regular intervals into airfields behind the battle area. The process can be likened to a conveyor belt extending from the point of departure to the final destination, with transport aircraft spaced along it at more or less equal intervals. The rate of flow of the airlift would be governed by the capabilities of the departure, en-route and arrival airfields to receive and park aircraft, to load and discharge their cargoes and to refuel them. It would be dangerous to have transport aircraft arrive at airfields near the war zone before those in front had been off-loaded and their loads moved away, thereby causing congestion and inviting attack from the enemy.

Similar principles would govern the operations by transport helicopters flying into areas immediately behind the land battle, as they moved forces and equipment into position as required by the army commander. The ability of helicopters to move troops and equipment in this way, far faster than is possible by any surface means and unhindered by surface obstacles such as rivers, marshy ground or hills, is a further important attribute of air power.

Modern air-to-surface weaponry

The past two decades have seen significant advances in the development of specialized types of air-to-surface weaponry. In previous chapters we have observed the extent to which the tactics of attack aircraft are dominated by the weapons they carry: Paveway laser-guided bombs, Durandel and JP233 airfield attack weapons, MW-1 area attack weapons, BL755 and other types of cluster bomb, TOW and Maverick anti-tank missiles, GAU-8 armour-piercing cannon, Shrike anti-radar missiles and Kormoran anti-ship missiles. Some of these weapons have been introduced only recently, the oldest is less than two decades old, and together they have brought about a huge improvement in the effectiveness of the attack aircraft. Those who have examined the available literature on air warfare might be surprised that the armoury of air-to-surface weapons available to NATO air forces is not vastly more diverse than it is.

A salient point to emerge from this analysis of air power is the degree of specialization now commonplace among air attack units in the Central European theatre. Two factors have caused this: first, the sheer cost of modern specialized aerial weapons, which prevents an attack squadron receiving anything like the full range of those its aircraft are theoretically capable of carrying; and second, the need for aircrews to concentrate the limited number of flying hours available in peacetime to train for a relatively narrow spread of missions – weapons dictate tactics and therefore the training necessary to use them to full effect. It is far easier to build multi-role aircraft than it is to train multi-role aircrews and keep them proficient.

Because of this specialization, during the initial phase of the conflict attack units would probably fly most of their sorties against the targets they were best equipped to engage and therefore best able to hit. F-111s and Tornadoes fitted with terrain-following radar and precise electronic navigation systems would mount most of their attacks by night or in poor weather. The most distant targets would be the prerogative of the F-111Es which, if they were attacking airfields, would use Durandel cratering bombs against runways; bridges and other small, hard targets would be dealt with by F-111Fs using Paveway laser-guided bombs; less-distant airfields would be hit by RAF Tornadoes using JP233 to close the runways and taxiways; concentrations of enemy vehicles behind the battle area would be attacked by German Air Force Tornadoes using the MW-1 area-attack weapon; enemy amphibious forces in the Baltic would be engaged by German Navy Tornadoes using Kormoran missiles. Short-range attack aircraft would mount attacks on enemy vehicle concentrations using cluster-bomb weapons like the British BL755. (Napalm has virtually passed out of use in most NATO air forces, not for humanitarian reasons but because cluster-bombs are more deadly against armoured vehicles than the spectacular but inaccurate fire-bombs.) A-10s would use Maverick missiles and high-velocity cannon to pick off individual enemy tanks and armoured vehicles in the battle area; and Lynx and other anti-tank helicopters would mount ambush attacks with TOW or HOT guided missiles on enemy armoured formations which had broken through the army's defensive line.

It may be stating the obvious, but whenever possible air commanders would use units against those targets which they were best able to engage; this would give the greatest possible number of targets destroyed for given numbers of sorties flown or aircraft lost, and would represent the most effective use of the available forces. The converse, to send aircraft to attack unsuitable targets or those for which their crews lacked the necessary specialist skills, equipment or weapons, would represent a far less effective use of resources and in extreme cases could result in attacks that cost more to mount than the damage they inflicted on the enemy. If one examines the history of air warfare it is amazing how often these basic rules have been ignored, or how often the air commanders who were aware of them have been overridden by political or military superiors who were not.

One problem is that the inexorable pressures of war itself could force air commanders away from their preferred course of action. Military experts agree that after a few days' all-out fighting several of the highly specialized types of aircraft weaponry would begin to run out. Such weapons are very expensive, which means that they are bought in far smaller numbers than their prospective users would wish. For example, the powerful MW-1 area-attack weapon carried by German Air Force Tornadoes costs more than £¾ million per container with sub-munitions, and after use the containers are jettisoned. The German Government has announced an order for 344 MW-1 systems for attacking enemy armour, or an average of about 1½ for each Tornado ordered for its Air Force. Certainly a series of well-executed attacks with that number of MW-1 containers would take an enormous toll of enemy vehicles, but it requires no great mathematical brain to work out how long its use could continue in a hard-fought conventional battle. There are similar shortages of other types of advanced weaponry. As stocks of specialized weapons became exhausted, attack aircraft would have to resort to the progressively greater use of general-purpose free-fall bombs, with a consequent reduction in effectiveness.

Electronic countermeasures

Electronic countermeasures are essential for the survival of aircraft that have to penetrate deep into enemy territory. Self-protection countermeasures – electronic jammers, radar warning receivers and dispensers for chaff (metalized strips to provide false targets on enemy radar) and flares (to decoy infra-red homing missiles) – are standard equipment on all F-111s, EF-111s, Tornadoes, F-15s, A-10s, RF-4Cs and F-4Gs. Such equipment is also carried by many but not all of the other attack aircraft.

Self-protection jamming would be radiated only when individual aircraft came under attack from radar-controlled weapons, to slow the engagement process and so give the aircraft time to escape by moving out of range. An aircraft flying at 600 knots covers 1.6 miles in 10 seconds, and if a radar lock-on can be delayed or broken for even half that time it could give an aircraft time to reach the next fold in the ground before missiles or shells could reach it. A combination of jamming, chaff and an evasive manoeuvre can be very effective in breaking the lock-on of an enemy fire-control radar. Provided they are released in good time, flares will decoy infra-red homing missiles safely clear of aircraft.

Jamming escort cover for attack forces would come from EF-111 aircraft, as described by Lieutenant-Colonel Vesely (Chapter 12). And 'hard kill' suppression of enemy missile defences would be provided by 'Wild Weasel' F-4 aircraft, as described by Lieutenant-Colonel Kersey (Chapter 13). Formations of attack aircraft lacking self-protection countermeasures equipment, and package formations attacking particularly important and heavily defended targets (as described in Chapter 1), would be the main recipients of such cover.

The other side

In considering the effectiveness of NATO air forces that would take part in an action in Central Europe, it should be borne in mind that there is a Soviet equivalent or near-equivalent for almost every type of Western combat aircraft. The new Flanker

fighter, believed designated the Su-27, probably has a performance similar to the F-15; the Fulcrum, believed designated the
MiG-29, is similar to the F-16. The Su-24 Fencer tactical attack
bomber is smaller than the F-111 but larger than the Tornado,
and is believed to carry a navigation and attack system with
capabilities similar to the F-111E (though probably not as good
as the F-111F or the Tornado). The MiG-23 and MiG-27
Flogger fighter-bombers are less effective than the F-16 but more
effective than some of the older types in use in NATO. The Su-25
Frogfoot attack aircraft appears to have been designed for close
air support operations similar to those flown by the A-10. NATO
combat aircraft have better radar and electronic systems than
their Soviet counterparts, and in most cases can carry a given
payload further. Some Yak-28 Brewer attack bombers have been
modified into jamming escort aircraft, and though it is doubtful
whether they would be as effective in this role as the EF-111 they
could still cause problems to the defenders. Although at the time
of writing such modern Soviet types as the Flanker, Fulcrum,
Fencer and Frogfoot equip only a small proportion of combat
units in Eastern Europe, these types are all in large-scale
production and in the future will replace several of the older
types. On top of that, of course, the Warsaw Pact air forces have
a considerable numerical superiority over those of NATO.

In attack helicopters the Warsaw Pact forces have the lead
both in quantity and in quality: the Mi-24 Hind is a much larger
and more effective battlefield helicopter than the Lynx or any
equivalent currently serving in Western Europe.

This author does not know whether the Soviets have weapons
in service equivalent to Paveway, Durandel, JP233, MW-1,
Maverick or Kormoran, or have aircraft equipped to perform the
'Wild Weasel' role. Without doubt they have the technological
capability to produce most or all of these, however, and it would
be prudent to assume that they have done so or are doing so.

From the foregoing it follows that in a conflict of the type
described, NATO F-15 fighters might find themselves trying to
block attacks by aircraft with many of the capabilities and
carrying weapons similar to those of the F-111 and Tornado,
perhaps supported by aircraft with some of the features of the
EF-111 and the F-4G. And NATO attack aircraft could find

themselves being engaged by fighters with performances similar to those of the F-15 and the F-16. The only certainty about a hard-fought slugging match of this sort, in which both sides possessed large quantities of sophisticated modern weapons and the determination to use them, is that both sides would suffer heavy losses in both men and equipment.

———————

This author has found a considerable measure of agreement within the NATO military hierarchy that a balance of power does exist between the two power blocs in Europe. Although the Warsaw Pact has a numerical superiority in conventional forces, the margin is not large enough to guarantee the success of an armoured thrust into the West contested by the full weight of NATO non-nuclear fire power. A major war in Europe fought with the panoply of modern conventional weapons would result in horrendous losses for both sides and would be accompanied by an inevitable drift towards a nuclear exchange that neither side could win. There is clear evidence that this view is held by the leaders of both power blocs. So long as this remains the case the conflict described on these pages will almost certainly remain confined within the realms of hypothesis.

Brief Details of Aircraft Types

A-10 Thunderbolt (Fairchild) US single-seat twin-engined armoured attack aircraft specially designed for the close air support role. Armament: one 30 mm high-velocity armour-piercing cannon plus up to six Maverick missiles. Take-off weight in combat configuration: 15 tons.

Alphajet (Dassault–Breguet–Dornier) Franco-German two-seat twin-engined aircraft, also used as an advanced trainer. In 2 ATAF the German Air Force operates two squadrons in the light attack role; and the Belgain Air Force operates one squadron in the visual reconnaissance role. One likely task for this highly manoeuvrable aircraft is to engage enemy helicopters. Armament: one 27 mm cannon and up to 3,000 lb of bombs. Take-off weight in combat configuration: about 6 tons.

Atlantic (Dassault–Breguet) Franco-German-Dutch-Italian multi-seat twin-turboprop long-range maritime reconnaissance and anti-submarine aircraft. Take-off weight in the combat configuration: about 40 tons.

Backfire NATO code-name for the Soviet Tupolev 26 twin-engined medium-range swing-wing reconnaissance bomber and maritime attack aircraft. Has been observed carrying various types of air-to-surface missile. Take-off weight in the combat configuration: about 100 tons.

Badger NATO code-name for the Soviet Tupolev 16 twin-engined medium-range bomber dating back to the 1950s. Still serving in the maritime reconnaissance and electronic warfare roles, and as a launch aircraft for anti-ship missiles. Take-off weight in the combat configuration: about 70 tons.

Blinder NATO code-name for the Soviet Tupolev 22 twin-engined medium-range supersonic reconnaissance bomber. Has been observed carrying various types of air-to-surface missile. Take-off weight in the combat configuration: about 85 tons.

Brewer NATO code-name for the Soviet Yakovlev 28 two-seat twin-engined attack bomber of 1960s vintage. Some have been converted into radar-jamming escort aircraft.

E-3 Sentry (Boeing) US four-engined airborne warning and control system aircraft based on the airframe of the Boeing 707 airliner. No armament. The flight crew is 4, with 13 radar controllers and technicians. Normal take-off weight in the operational configuration: about 135 tons.

EC-130 C-130 Hercules four-propjet transport aircraft modified for the communications jamming role; equipment code-named 'Compass Call'.

EF-111 Raven (General Dynamics) US radar-jamming escort aircraft modified from the F-111 attack aircraft.

F-4 Phantom (McDonnell Douglas) US two-seat twin-engined multi-purpose combat aircraft. Operated by the Royal Air Force in the long-range interceptor role, by the German Air Force in the fighter-bomber role, by the USAF and the German Air Force in the reconnaissance role and by the USAF in the 'Wild Weasel' role. Take-off weight in the combat configuration: about 23 tons.

F-15 Eagle (McDonnell Douglas) US single-seat twin-engined night and all-weather air superiority fighter, capable of supersonic speed at all altitudes. Armament: one 20 mm cannon, four AIM-7 Sparrow missiles, four AIM-9 Sidewinder missiles. Take-off weight in combat configuration: just over 25 tons.

F-16 Fighting Falcon (General Dynamics) US-designed single-seat single-engined fighter-bomber. In 2 ATAF operated in the Dutch and Belgian Air Forces. Armament: one 20 mm cannon; can carry four AIM-9L missiles in the interceptor role; can carry up to 4,000 lb of bombs on an attack mission. Dutch Air Force operates one squadron of F-16s in the reconnaissance role. Take-off weight in the combat configuration: about 12 tons.

F-111 (General Dynamics) US two-seat twin-engined swing-wing heavyweight night and all-weather tactical attack bomber, normal bomb load up to 8,000 lb. Take-off weight in combat configuration: just under 40 tons.

Fencer NATO code-name for the Soviet Sukhoi 24 two-seat twin-engined swing-wing all-weather heavy tactical attack bomber. Believed to have a full night and all-weather attack capability. Take-off weight in combat configuration: estimated at about 35 tons.

Flanker NATO code-name for the latest Soviet single-seat twin-engined air superiority fighter, believed to be designated the Sukhoi 27, similar in size and performance to the F-15.

Flogger NATO code-name for the Soviet MiG-23 and MiG-27 single-seat single-engined swing-wing aircraft: MiG-23 is air-to-air fighter, MiG–27 is air-to-ground attack. Take-off weight in combat configuration: estimated at about 17 tons.

Foxbat NATO code-name for the Soviet MiG-25 single-seat twin-engined high-altitude high-speed interceptor fighter. Take-off weight in the combat configuration: estimated at about 35 tons.

Frogfoot NATO code-name for the Soviet Sukhoi 25 single-seat twin-engined armoured attack aircraft designed for the close air support role and similar in its characteristics to the A-10. Take-off weight in the combat configuration: estimated at about 16 tons.

Gazelle (Westland) Anglo-French single-engined lightweight general-purpose helicopter. When operated by the British Army in the battlefield reconnaissance role carries a crew of two and no armament; take-off weight in this configuration: about 1½ tons.

Harrier (British Aerospace) British single-seat single-engined light attack and reconnaissance aircraft, capable of vertical take-off and landing. Armament: two 30 mm cannon and up to five BL755 cluster bombs. Usual take-off weight in combat configuration: about 10 tons; but at that weight a short ground run is necessary before it can become airborne.

Hawk (British Aerospace) British two-seat single-engined advanced trainer. Can be operated in the daylight interceptor role with two AIM-9 Sidewinder missiles, flown as a single-seater; in this configuration the take-off weight is about 5½ tons.

Hind NATO code-name for the Soviet MIL-24 twin-engined large armed assault helicopter. Has appeared in various versions: as an armed transport carrying up to eight troops; as a ground attack helicopter equipped for night and all-weather operations; and as an anti-tank helicopter. Weight in combat configuration: estimated at 10 tons.

Jaguar (SEPECAT) Anglo-French single-seat twin-engined attack aircraft, almost entirely superseded in 2 ATAF by the Tornado. At the time of writing one RAF squadron in Germany operates this type in the reconnaissance role. Take-off weight in the combat configuration: about 13 tons.

Lightning (English Electric) British single-seat twin-engined night and all-weather high-altitude interceptor. Armament: two 30 mm cannon and two Firestreak or Red Top infra-red homing missiles. Take-off weight in the combat configuration: about 22 tons. Due to be phased out of service in 1988 and replaced by the Tornado F.3.

Lynx (Westland) Anglo-French twin-engined general-purpose helicopter. When operated by the British Army in the anti-tank role it carries a crew of two and eight TOW missiles. Take-off weight in the combat configuration: just over 3 tons.

Mirage 5 (Dassault) French single-seat single-engined attack aircraft, operated in 2 ATAF by the Belgian Air Force. That force also operates one squadron of these aircraft in the reconnaissance role. Take-off weight in combat configuration: about 11 tons.

NF-5 Version of the Northrop F-5 Freedom Fighter, built under licence in Holland. Single-seat twin-engined attack aircraft operated in 2 ATAF by the Dutch Air Force. Take-off weight in combat configuration: about 9 tons.

Tornado (Panavia) Anglo-German-Italian two-seat twin-engined swing-wing aircraft. Within 2 ATAF operated by the Royal Air Force and the German Air Force. The GR1 is the air-to-ground attack version; the F2 and F3 are long-range air-to-air interceptor versions operated only by the RAF. Armament (GR1): two 27 mm cannon, up to 8,000 lb of bombs, two AIM–9 Sidewinder missiles; (F2 and F3): one 27 mm cannon, four Skyflash missiles, four AIM-9 Sidewinder missiles. Take-off weight in the combat configuration: about 27 tons.

Glossary

Aggressor Training programme in air-to-air combat initiated by the US Air Force, employing aircraft types and tactics similar to those employed by Warsaw Pact forces.

AIM-7 Sparrow US medium-range radar semi-active-homing air-to-air missile.

AIM-9 Sidewinder US short-range infra-red homing air-to-air missile, widely used throughout NATO.

AWACS Airborne Warning and Control System. See E-3 Sentry aircraft.

BL755 British cluster bomb weapon containing 147 armour-piercing bomblets.

Blowpipe British short-range shoulder-launched command-guided surface-to-air weapon.

BVR Beyond Visual Range. The engagement of enemy aircraft from distances where visual identification is not possible.

Chaff Metalized strips released from aircraft or fired into the sky by rockets, intended to confuse enemy radars by providing false targets.

Chaperral US short-range battlefield surface-to-air missile, employing infra-red homing.

Clock Code System used to indicate other aircraft horizontally, relative to the nose of the aircraft. 12 o'clock is dead ahead, 6 o'clock is dead astern, 3 o'clock and 9 o'clock are to the right and left respectively.

Close Air Support Air operations against enemy land forces in close proximity with friendly forces. Because of the risk of hitting friendly forces, such operations would be directed by a forward air controller on the ground or in a helicopter.

'Compass Call' Communications jamming equipment fitted to EC-130 aircraft.

Counter-Air Those operations mounted against the opposing air force. Offensive counter-air operations comprise attacks on airfields, surface-to-air missile sites and ground facilities associated with the enemy air force. Defensive counter-air operations comprise air defence operations to protect friendly territory and forces, by fighter aircraft and surface-to-air weapons systems.

'Dumb' bomb Non-guided bomb.

Durandel French runway cratering weapon, carried by USAF F-111 and other aircraft.

EWO Electronic Warfare Officer. Crewman in EF-111s and F-4Gs who operates the electronic warfare systems carried in the aircraft.

FAC Forward Air Controller. Directs close air support missions in the battle area from a position on the ground or in a helicopter.

FEBA Forward Edge of the Battle Area.

FLOT Forward Line of Own Troops.

Fratricide Unintentional destruction of friendly aircraft or other systems by friendly weapons.

Green Flag Elaborate and realistic aircrew training programme initiated by the US Air Force, in which tactical exercises are flown in Nevada against simulated air defence weapons systems employed by Warsaw Pact forces.

Hawk US medium-range semi-active radar-homing surface-to-air missile system, optimized for the engagement of low-flying aircraft. Deployed in large numbers in Europe.

HOT Short-range wire-guided anti-tank missile, carried by armoured vehicles and some helicopters.

IFF Identification Friend or Foe. Electronic system fitted to all combat aircraft, which answers interrogating signals with a coded reply to identify the aircraft as friendly.

Interdiction Air attacks on enemy supplies and reinforcements moving towards the battle area, before they come into contact with friendly forces. Typically such attacks would be mounted against targets in a zone between 10 km and 100 km in front of friendly forces. Interdiction attacks can be subdivided into Battlefield Air Interdiction missions (against targets relatively close to the battlefield) and Deep Interdiction missions (against targets further back).

'Iron bomb' Non-nuclear bomb.

JP233 British airfield denial weapon, carried by RAF Tornado aircraft.

Kormoran German radar-homing sea-skimming anti-ship missile, carried by German Navy Tornado and F-104 aircraft.

Laydown Bombing Technique for very low altitude attack, in which the aircraft passes close over the target and releases bombs fitted with parachutes or other retardation systems, to give the releasing aircraft time to get clear before they detonate.

Maple Flag NATO tactical training exercise, similar to Green Flag (q.v.), flown over northern Canada.

MW-1 German area attack weapon carried by German Air Force Tornado aircraft.

Nike US long-range radar command-guided surface-to-air missile system, for use against aircraft flying at medium- or high-altitude.

Pave Tack US external pod fitted with infra-red sensing and laser designation equipment, carried under the fuselages of USAF F-111F attack aircraft and RF-4C reconnaissance aircraft.

Paveway US laser-guided bomb for precision attack operations. Homes on laser energy reflected off the target; can be used in conjunction with Pave Tack designator (q.v.).

Rapier British short-range command-guided surface-to-air missile system used in large numbers by British forces.

Red Flag US tactical training exercise, similar to Green Flag.

SA-4 NATO designation for a Soviet medium-range surface-to-air missile system, with missile launchers and separate missile control radar mounted on tracked vehicles to enable it to be deployed close behind the battle area. First revealed in 1964.

SA-6 NATO designation for a more advanced surface-to-air missile system than the SA-4 with a much better capability against low-flying aircraft. Missile launchers and separate missile control radar mounted on tracked vehicles. First revealed in 1967. Proved very effective during the Arab–Israeli war in 1973.

SA-7 NATO designation for an infantry shoulder-launched infra-red homing surface-to-air missile, deployed in large numbers.

SA-8 NATO designation for a short-range surface-to-air missile system with missile launchers and missile control radar mounted on the same six-wheeled overland vehicle. Optimized for the engagement of low-flying aircraft, probably similar in capability to the British Rapier system. First revealed in 1975.

SA-9 NATO designation for a short-range surface-to-air missile system, employing a missile believed similar to the SA-7 launched from a modified armoured scout car. First revealed in 1975.

Skyflash British radar semi-active-homing air-to-air missile, carried by RAF Phantom and Tornado fighters.

TEREC Tactical Electronic REConnaissance system. Passive radar receiving system fitted to the RF-4C reconnaissance aircraft for the location of enemy radar sites.

Toss-Bombing Technique in which bombs are released while the aircraft is in (usually) a shallow climb at high speed. The bombs' trajectory then carries them several miles before they hit the ground. Though not as accurate as laydown bombing (q.v.), toss-bombing has the advantage that the aircraft does not have to fly directly over the target.

TOW Tube-launched, Optically tracked, Wire-guided missile. Short-range anti-tank missile carried by Lynx and other helicopters, also used by infantry.

Weapon Systems Officer Crewman in multi-seat combat aircraft who navigates the aircraft and operates its attack systems.

'Wild Weasel' Code name for USAF units specially trained and equipped to mount attacks on enemy ground radars and surface-to-air defensive sytems.

ZSU 23-4 Soviet short-range anti-aircraft system, with four 23 mm cannon and a fire control radar mounted on the same tracked vehicle. Deployed in large numbers in Warsaw Pact armies.

Index